"LISTEN I'm Still Here"

The Continuation of Love
From the Other Side
PART I

By Dorothy and Jack Farley

Balboa Press books may be ordered through booksellers or by contacting:

Balboa Press
A Division of Hay House
1663 Liberty Drive
Bloomington, IN 47403
www.balboapress.com
1-(877) 407-4847

Because of the dynamic nature of the Internet, any web addresses or links contained in this book may have changed since publication and may no longer be valid. The views expressed in this work are solely those of the author and do not necessarily reflect the views of the publisher, and the publisher hereby disclaims any responsibility for them.

The author of this book does not dispense medical advice or prescribe the use of any technique as a form of treatment for physical, emotional, or medical problems without the advice of a physician, either directly or indirectly. The intent of the author is only to offer information of a general nature to help you in your quest for emotional and spiritual well-being. In the event you use any of the information in this book for yourself, which is your constitutional right, the author and the publisher assume no responsibility for your actions.

Any people depicted in stock imagery provided by Thinkstock are models, and such images are being used for illustrative purposes only.
Certain stock imagery © Thinkstock.

Printed in the United States of America

ISBN: 978-1-4525-4440-3 (sc)
ISBN: 978-1-4525-4441-0 (hc)
ISBN: 978-1-4525-4439-7 (e)
Library of Congress Control Number: 2011963386
Balboa Press rev. date: 02/02/2012

ALL PROCEEDS FROM THE SALE OF THIS BOOK
GO TO CAT HAVEN CHARITABLE TRUST, RESORT
FOR CATS & WILDLIFE PRESERVE: OUR MISSION
AND PASSION TO MAKE THIS WORLD A BETTER
PLACE. OUR LOVE FOR THE ANIMAL KINGDOM
WILL REMAIN OUR BLISS FOR ETERNITY.

Cat Haven
Charitable Trust

P.O. Box 150022
Austin, Texas 78715

Resort For Cats
& Wildlife Preserve

"Listen, I'm Still Here"

— The Continuation of Love From the Other Side

Cover illustration painted by Jack Farley in the early '80s — "HEAVEN"...as he saw it.

ACKNOWLEDGMENTS & BIBLIOGRAPHY

We are pleased to acknowledge permission to reprint brief quotations from the following works.

"The Divine Plan." Unity Magazine. Unity Church, Unity Village, Missouri. (Reprinted with permission of Unity®.)

Colleen Zuck, Ed. "Daily Lesson, July 31, 1988, Sunday." Daily Word: Silent Unity's Magazine, July 1988. Unity School of Christianity, Unity Village, Missouri. (Reprinted with permission of Unity®, publisher of Daily Word®.)

A Course In Miracles. Tiburon, California: Foundation for Inner Peace, © 1975.

Louise L. Hay. Heal Your Body. Santa Monica, California: Hay House, Inc., © 1988.

Journey of Souls: Case Studies of Life Between Lives by Michael Newton, Ph.D. © 1994, Fifth Revised Edition. © 2005. Llewellyn Worldwide, Ltd., 2143 Wooddale Drive, Woodbury, MN 55125-2989. Used by permission and with the best wishes of the publisher. All rights reserved.

Doug Manning. Continuing Care Series. Oklahoma City: In-Sight Books, © 2002.

Prem Rawat. An undated speech.

Dedication:

This book is written in memory of and to honor my one true love, Jack Farley — my partner in many lifetimes, husband and masterful companion in this one.

Life was a continuous stream of miracles with Jack by my side. His patience, unselfishness, teachings of love, wisdom, and allowing me to "be me" were priceless gifts he gave and continues to give from the other side — his new dimension. We still have conversations and work together channeling healing energy to make this world a better place...

The life we live is God's — He is in charge. When we allow time to listen for God's direction, we may also hear the voices of our loved ones who have seemingly left us. They are with us always, just in a different realm. They want us to know they are still here, and they want us to listen.

Such is the case with my beloved Jack. On March 30, 2007, he died in my arms while we were dancing. What a way to go!

Audrey Hunt — my spiritual teacher and intuitive (psychic) in Glendale, Arizona — sees people's spirits lined up, wrapping around the world waiting patiently to bring messages to loved ones. There are so few people on earth who are open to receiving messages in a pure way and not putting their own interpretations on them. Most spirits want to come back and say how sorry they are for things left undone or unsaid. I am one of the lucky ones because Jack and I talk whenever I open myself. We are always working partners, and this continues while he is at a higher level.

GRATITUDE TO:

- God.
- Jack — my beloved who taught me to love myself, to know God, and that things only get better.
- Rose and Leslie Beckley, my parents. I believe they were my choice. They accepted the challenge and always did their best.
- Lewis Jackson, for bringing me to America.
- Dr. Robert Michael Jackson, for allowing me to feel pride as the mother of a doctor.
- Dr. Mike Huneycutt, my first guide to the innate.
- Paul and Lisa Lin, for their healing and cleansing techniques.
- Jim Kane, my first self-worth acknowledger.
- Rev. Mark Yarnell, for prophetic spiritual inspiration.
- Ritchie Mintz, a healer and genuine loving friend of 25 years.
- Phyliss Mangold, for her loyalty at my lowest times and friendship for 20 years.
- Datha Farrington — spiritual therapist, astrologer, and longtime friend.
- Audrey Hunt — intuitive teacher, supporter, and friend for for over 25 years.
- Kay Stahli, my silent interpreter, and distant supporter.
- Yong Cui, for his wisdom, grace, and healing skills.
- Paul A. Minar, a new inspring friend and numerologist.
- Robin Krier, a woman's woman, totally loving and beautiful.
- Dr. Douglas Stakes, Janet Stakes, and Vi Michler, for healing and support.
- Alan Mesher, author and healer, for introducing me to Ching Li and releasing my mother's energy.
- Don Walden, the Trust attorney and personal friend.
- Shakti Miller, healer and inspiration. It was her suggestion that I write this book.
- Everyone I have ever known or met who gave me a breath of love and all of those good people in between.

SPECIAL GRATITUDE TO SHAKTI MILLER, AUDREY HUNT, KAY STAHLI, AND PAUL A. MINAR. WITHOUT THEIR CONTRIBUTIONS TO MY AWARENESS, THIS BOOK COULD NOT HAVE BEEN WRITTEN.

The Divine Plan

For each of us there is a divine plan for our lives and for our spiritual unfoldment, a plan established and lovingly overseen by our Heavenly Father. This divine plan includes many lessons we have to learn to develop our spiritual understanding many bountiful blessings to enrich and enhance our lives and, finally, an ultimate goal — conscious oneness with the Father. Though we may not perceive precisely how or why our individual plan is unfolding as it is, we can know that God is in charge of it and that it is proceeding exactly as it should.

With this in mind we can be less fearful of our future, less resistant to unexpected changes in our plans, less self-pitying about our problems, and less overwhelmed by the task of attaining spiritual mastery. We can know that an ordered plan — not sheer chaos or the whims of a capricious God — rules our lives. We can also be assured that this plan is for our benefit, our highest good, our greatest happiness. It is not designed to test or to frighten or defeat us. God's will is for us to mature and be perfected as His sons and daughters, but God knows that in order to accomplish this we must learn some lessons that may seem difficult or confusing to us.

Friends, we need to agree — not just submit — to the divine plan God has set in motion for our lives. God knows exactly what we must do to receive the greatest growth and blessings. Let us, then, place our trust and expectation in God and accept that what is happening through us (not to us!) is a part of God's gracious and perfect divine plan for us.

INTRODUCTION

No one knows – absolutely no one knows – what effort it takes to put food onto a plate and then hardly be able to raise a fork while grieving tears blind your eyes, your breathing is stifled, and your continuously throbbing heart feels as though it has fallen into the stomach's pit. No one knows unless he/she has lost a loved one too. My younger husband to whom I had been married nearly 20 years was gone, and a more perfect cosmic relationship could not have existed. We were connected at the heart with familiarity, comfort, and a sense of similar passion to make the world a better place. We had found our purpose-driven life together, and for me it was now shattered.

I was alone – despondent and a little angry – with no family and few available friends. I proceeded to overwork myself physically, mentally, and emotionally for five months to maintain the life my husband and I had known; but I was also just beginning to know God as I wailed and questioned the loss of my beloved. One evening I shouted and pleaded to God that I wanted to talk to my husband's spirit. Then came the quiet answer: "You are." Thus began the conversations.

How did I get here? How did I get to this point where I could communicate with my deceased beloved? I began to reflect – to remember the path I had taken, the spiritual search and journey of a life unfinished but reaching fulfillment.

TABLE OF CONTENTS

CHAPTER 1

GOODBYE
TO
CONTROL

ILLUMINATION

*Nobody has any experience in their life that they
don't need for their personal growth.*

*Every moment of your day when you are in
the presence of another you have the opportunity to
increase your movement
toward enlightenment.*

On June 21, 1935, I made my grand entrance at four pounds and one ounce into a modest bedroom at 34 Monson Road, London, England. A midwife delivered me two months premature. I am told that I wanted to get on with life, and I have not stopped in the last 72 years. A Gemini on the cusp of Cancer can do many things at the same time, all with a nurturing heart.

My formative years as a child endured the bombing of London in World War II, the 1941 blitz. It was a time when everyone, including children, obeyed rules and carried mandatory gas masks. Discipline, discipline, discipline was a matter of life or death. Everyone had to learn to follow instructions and do as told. Obedience was an essential part of life. To this day, I have great difficulty when I witness disobedience in children because following rules was my childhood foundation.

During the war, absolutely everything was rationed – from foods to fabrics to clothes to candy ("sweets" in England). I had a grandmother who did not care too much for sweets and therefore gave her ration coupons to my mother. I loved my grandmother! I would sit at her knees whenever she visited because I knew this was where the extra sweets came from.

Two ounces of corned beef per week per ration book was all the meat we had for the longest time. These days, this is the average amount that a person puts in a sandwich for lunch. My mother cooked up some unique meals with corned beef as a base, but now I can't bear the smell of it.

Mummy was a first-class seamstress and worked for a lady named Dorothy Buckmaster – thus my name, Dorothy. Mummy could make something tasteful from a corn sack. There was a season when she had saved clothing coupons to buy fabric and make us both winter clothes, but somewhere, somehow her handbag and clothing coupons were stolen. Mummy's distressful response was nothing short of alarming; and as a result of not being able to buy new fabric, her only alternative was to let the seams out and hems down of existing clothing. Fortunately, we had little vanity in those days; we only had pride in what we learned to overcome. There was a definite pulling together and sharing by family members and neighbors. Those *were* the "good old days," in spite of shortages and restrictions.

I can remember not having enough teeth in my comb to comb my long red hair. A knock came at the door one day and the next-door neighbor told Mummy, "Mrs. Beckley, they have combs at Woolworth's." Mummy swiftly put a bonnet on my head, and we almost ran to Woolworth's. There was a long line (a "queue"), but we waited our turn to buy the new combs. You can imagine the simplicity of the occurrence, but it was a special occasion for us. I came home and immediately wanted to throw the fragment of the old comb away. Alas, Mummy wouldn't allow it. "You never know when you might need it," she said. I never understood her thinking on this, but that was my mother.

There are, of course, many more memories of the war. I remember walking home from school with a friend, whom – unbeknownst to me – I would never see again because her house was bombed that night. It surprises me now, how fragmented our fear appeared to be on the surface. Little did I know that putting on a happy face was not a solution for the fear but merely a temporary bandage for the symptoms, symptoms that would catch up with us later in life.

After war broke out, the beautiful London parks became allotments, which were large sections of land divided into small pieces for people to rent and grow vegetables. This is what my father did, and every night he and I would walk a mile or so to a local park and tend to the growing produce on his allotment. I can still remember the excitement when it was time to harvest a few potatoes. Remarkably, no one ever thought of taking from another person's garden; it never entered our minds. There was respect for our neighbors and congratulations if, for example, their sweet peas were more succulent than ours. What a difference in the times then and now.

At the beginning of the war, there were reinforced concrete steel shelters built by the government in the streets, but they soon became foul and unusable. People young and old abused them as if they were toilets, so we had to resort to taking care of ourselves.

When I was 7 years old, we had a steel shelter constructed at our home. At first, we had our back garden dug out and lined with concrete. Then a corrugated steel roof was placed on top and covered with the dirt. The construction meant we had to go down steep steps to sit inside this cold concrete-lined space. The first night we used it, Mummy fell down the steps because it was dark and the lanterns were inadequate. After that, I assume Mummy and the upstairs neighbors got together and decided to build another form of shelter. This time it was inside the home, and I believe this inside shelter was called an

Anderson shelter. Mummy and I lived downstairs in a self-contained apartment ("flatlet"), and it must have been our duty to share this new shelter space with the people who lived upstairs. My bedroom, where the shelter was constructed, was not much more than an eight-by-eight space. As a child, I was the only person in this shelter (which had a twin-size mattress as a foundation to sit on) who was able to sit upright. Mummy, the parents from upstairs, their two children, and I spent almost every night in this space for a year or more, from sunset to sunrise. It was cramped beyond description, but we felt safe together. We had cookies ("biscuits") to eat and a Thermos of warm milk, and we always made jokes and tried to laugh. Daddy at the time was in the British Royal Air Force somewhere, so Mummy was in charge. Little did I know how scared she was and how she hid her fears to protect me.

At school during the air raids we children went single file down into a basement that had no bathrooms. All we had were huge steel milk urns behind a curtain: one for the boys and the other one for the girls. The echo from the urn while peeing was so embarrassing for me that I refused to use it. I believe this is why I suffered from bladder problems later in life.

When I go back in my memories, I see only houses with windows boarded up because every window had to be covered with wood to protect from falling or broken glass, similar to the anticipation of a hurricane in the United States. Also, light was absolutely not allowed to show. If the German planes flying over saw light, they would pinpoint it as a destination for bombing. You couldn't even have a flashlight unless it had mesh netting to diffuse the output. Air raid wardens walked the streets at night. It was their duty to call to you and knock on your door if you had failed to cover a window completely.

During the height of London blitz bombing, Mummy and I were evacuated from London to the country, Wimborne in Dorset. Daddy found the location. Country folks opened their homes to Londoners, and the Langford family gave us a wonderful welcome. The aroma of hot apple cake filled the farmhouse the day we moved in and sat down to eat our first country meal, which was indescribably delicious. The Langfords had chickens; consequently, they had eggs, which were a rarity in London. (On occasion Mummy had bought eggs on the black market. I didn't understand as a child that to accomplish this, she had to pay a high price.) Also, on the farm the amount of produce was considerably more than what had come from Daddy's allotment. The Langfords had a wide variety of apple, pear, and peach trees in their orchard. Blackberries and nuts grew wild along the country lanes where we could pick as many as we wanted. Sometimes Mr. Langford took us out early in the morning to pick mushrooms for breakfast.

The country schoolhouse had only 20 children, which meant 10 per classroom, all ages! This was a major change from the London classrooms where there would be 30 or more per class of the same age. I loved it.

Though most of my memories of country life are good, I have one painful recollection. I had learned to milk a cow named Smiley, who was my favorite. One day at dinner while eating, Mr. Langford commented on "how tender Smiley was."

When I realized that Smiley was my dinner, I left the table in tears.

Mummy remained friends with the Langford family for the rest of her life. She would vacation in Wimborne on occasion and tell me how they were doing. We were so fortunate to have found these kind people who opened their hearts to us, and this sharing experience profoundly influenced my life.

§

London was dark for a long time. Busses had only dim lights, and the windows were covered with a web-like fabric to prevent glass from falling everywhere if shattered. After the war when all these restrictions were removed, we could "see the light" of the city and it was thrilling beyond description. I remember the day the war was over and all the rejoicing. I walked with Mummy and my aunt and cousins for miles (because there was little public transportation that day) to get to Trafalgar Square and celebrate the end of this disastrous period. Afterwards on the walk home, I remember seeing the sunrise and everyone on the street smiling and kissing each other. When I close my eyes, I can still smell and feel the energy of that day's grand excitement.

At the end of the war, we began to take walking tours as a family (again, public transportation was limited) to the center of London to observe the destruction and devastation from the bombings. It truly looked like the end of the world, but somehow over time London emerged from the rubble and was miraculously rebuilt.

England soon received food imports again – particularly fruits and vegetables, many of which I had never seen. In fact, I had never eaten a banana until I was 11 years old, and it was a thrill to go to the grocery store with Mummy to purchase one. We split the banana three ways: for Mummy, Daddy, and myself. This memory remains so strong that, to this day, all I can eat is about a 1/3 of a banana.

During the rebuilding process, some theatres reopened. For me it was a big thrill to go to the theatre. My parents, aunt, uncle, and cousins went to our first live theatre show together. (I had gone to the Pantomimes, which were live children's shows such as *Peter Pan*, when I was 4 or 5. My godmother, Aunt Grace, always took her nieces and nephews for our Christmas treat.) One night my family took the bus and then walked to the outside of the theatre to buy our tickets for the least expensive seats. The seats were so high up they were known as in "The Gods." It was great. We were all excited waiting in the queue, we had a box of chocolates to share (a custom for theatre-goers in England at the time), and life was good.

I have a strong memory before the show of an enormous black stretch limo driving up outside the theatre doors. A fully uniformed chauffeur got out and walked around to the street side where I was standing. He opened the limo door and inside I saw an extremely handsome young man lying on a stretcher. He was wheeled up the steps into the theatre. Later I saw inside that he was situated close to the front row. At the young age of 11, I realized at that moment how happy I was *to be me*. You might call this a pivotal life experience. I could *walk up* the stairs all the way into "The Gods," and in my mind I said over and over again how thankful I was to be me. I already understood the value of good health and that I would always do everything

I could in my life to remain healthy. (In fact, my passion for maintaining good health and it being *my* responsibility has actually consumed a good portion of my life.)

§

We are what we believe and what we believe we are. And we are all monsters – whether good or bad – of our own making because of how we think, our beliefs, and putting our beliefs into action.

My understanding is that we choose our parents before we are born. Our souls know the lessons we need to learn this time around, so we hook up with or come through those who will illustrate to us the lessons we need to master. For example, the father I chose in this lifetime was humorous, sweet, very loving of my mother and me, and especially caring of children. He was both giving and allowing. But in my maturing years I saw that he was possibly too allowing of my mother. She made every decision – for example, what he should eat, how much he should eat, and when he should eat! My mother made every decision that she could in my life also, even for my first marriage. The exception at that time was my wedding dress; she allowed me to select with her specific suggestions. Because of my mother's experience and gift at sewing, she created a lace masterpiece for me, yet she didn't share who was coming to the wedding. It took years until I finally learned to say enough to my mother on her insistence of how I should live my life. The sparks flew when I at long last in my 40s dared to speak up for myself, and she became furious and then apparently fainted. (This was over the phone, as I was in the US and she in England.)

My mother did not communicate with me for months after this exchange. She never told me that she loved me until I was 48 years old, and then only in a letter, in which she later added, "Oops, there I said it."

I believe that in my attempts to please my mother, I became rather obsessive about cleaning because this was something I could control in my life with perfection. I have always taken care of everything I own; for example, I have a couple of 20-year-old dresses that still look brand new. I always tried to get everything "good enough" for my mother. What a beating we take emotionally – even in middle age or older – when we allow others to have power over us!

My mother talked down to me even when I was in my 60s. One year, upon arriving to visit her with Jack after a 6,000-mile trip to England amid bad weather and London railroad strikes, my mother waved her walking cane and greeted me with: "Where have you been?" I replied, "Nice to see you too, mother." (Jack was shocked at her attitude although I had become accustomed to it.) I can laugh now, wish my mother peace, and assure her she is forgiven. I hope she has learned to forgive me as well. As parents we have a life-altering responsibility to our children; when we are young, we sometimes do not honor this. It is only when we mature and look back at the patterns and teachings we continued from our parents that we see our mother or father's influence in our own behavior. Sad. When all the things we have been told we cannot do or should not do are so deeply imbedded in our psyches, we are blinded to what we are able to do and do well.

My first husband was a handsome man, bronzed from the sunshine of South Africa, where he had been stationed with the American Air Force as a radio operator. The night I met him, he had just returned from South Africa and was in London for the weekend, TDY (Temporary Duty). Though his birthplace was in England, he grew up in the US. I first met him at the Lyceum Theatre in London when dancing and big bands were popular for young people in the 1950s. This theatre had been converted to a ballroom with theatre seats removed, a beautiful dance floor installed, and a large crystal ball suspended from the ceiling. There were tables for two or four with dainty lights set on the balconies where you could sit, enjoy a drink and companionship, and watch the dancers below. It was very romantic.

I loved dancing and had learned to ballroom dance at an all-girl high school when I was around age 14. My friend Sheila – who had earned bronze, silver, and gold medallions for ballroom dancing – taught others and me. During lunch breaks we would go into the school gymnasium where the floor was perfect for dancing, and Sheila would show us how to correctly do the steps. While she did the gentlemen steps, she would teach us the ladies steps. It was so much fun. When I was 16 and able to go to large dancehalls in London – they were huge and formal in those days – I would dance every Saturday night. I always showed up early because I had to be home early. My deadline for being home was always the same, and I had to stick to it. At 11:00 o'clock my father would be in his pajamas peering behind the sitting room curtain window at anybody who brought me home.

One evening I was at the Lyceum dancehall – I was then 18 – with my friend Jeanette and saw this handsome man walking down the stairs. I remember exactly what he was wearing and how magnificent he looked. I told Jeanette, "I'm going to marry that man." He was apparently watching me too. In those days it was totally inappropriate for a woman to ask a man to dance, but on this particular night it seemed easy for me. I walked over to my future husband and asked, "Would you think me terribly rude if I asked you to dance?" He smiled and said, "No, I was just plucking up the courage to ask you." And that's how we met.

An early memory of our relationship was during one of his weekend trips to London in the summertime. Summers in London can be quite cool, and he was wearing a topcoat. I remember him telling me that if he were in Austin, Texas, he would be swimming in Barton Springs and that it would be 100 degrees. I thought, "Oh sure, typical American boasting." Though having lived in Texas for over 30 years now, I know only too well he was telling the truth!

In 1954 he was to be discharged from the US Air Force and return to the States. By then I was 20, we knew we wanted to get married, but it was generally understood in England at the time that a young woman didn't get married until she was 21. So one weekend we planned to ask my father's permission at dinner. My father intuitively knew the question was coming, was nervously shaking, and said emphatically, "NO." He said it would be too hard on my mother. You can imagine our disappointment, but my folks did not trust this Yank to provide for me and thought he would vanish in a few months. Well, he didn't, and even though we were separated for a year, we still planned our marriage – or rather, my mother planned our marriage – for August 7, 1955.

In those days airfare was out of the question, so a year in advance we booked passage on a small Greek cruise ship to bring my husband-to-be to England from the US. After the ship stopped in England, it continued to Greece while we were married in London. A week after my husband's arrival, the ship came back to England, and we boarded it on its return to the US.

Back then, visas for entry into the US were limited, and the paper work was time consuming. After the wedding I had yet to complete my entry visa; but because I was now married to an American, it was easier with my husband as my sponsor. The journey on the ship was our honeymoon, and I was terribly seasick during the 14-day trip. The Atlantic Ocean can be a beast in August, especially with hurricanes stirring it up. The day we pulled into the harbor in New York City, Ms. Liberty witnessed the skirt of my beautiful shantung suit fall to the floor. During the course of the trip, I had lost so much weight that I needed a safety pin to hold up my skirt. In New York it was 92 degrees, which is something I had never experienced. The perspiration from my underarms revealed a huge stain on my suit jacket. What a mess I was to greet my new family! On the dockside while waiting for the unloading of the ship, I enjoyed my first jelly doughnut. Because I didn't know about the fruit filling, I got strawberry jelly on my new suit. Nonetheless, I remained carefree because I was in America, which was something I had dreamed of since I was 14 years old. I would watch Doris Day movies as a teenager and imagine what it would be like to live in the US. I can remember telling my father, "One day I am going to America." His was not a happy response!

My first husband and I were married for 25 years, and there were many good times. However, through the years, our differences became more evident. I wasn't happy with my marriage or myself. I felt like a failure as a wife and mother, and I attempted something drastic. However, at this time I received my very first message that I knew to be from God: ***"HOW COULD YOU BE SO SELFISH TO DENY YOUR SON HIS MOTHER?"***

This was another pivotal point and a wake up call. My soul had begun to evolve. Because my mother had been so controlling, I never learned the lesson of standing up for myself and my values, so I continued to attract the same controlling energy in a husband. Somehow I had gone from the frying pan into the fire and didn't even know it.

My first marriage produced one son, Robert, who is brilliant like his father and with whom I am well pleased, for he never gave me one moment of trouble. Robert's brain worked so fast as a child that during school he would finish assignments before the rest of his fellow students. Often, children with so much energy find themselves occupying time with troublesome activities, but not my son – he had set out at an early age to make himself of value. Robert graduated in the top two percent of his class from The University of Texas-Houston School of Dermatology and was the dermatology student of the year when he graduated in the early '80s. At that point, I knew my duty as a mother raising him was over. I needed to start thinking about myself.

I soon began to enjoy a deep sense of exuberance through my spiritual learning experiences. I wanted to share, but this was not well received at home. It was obvious that I had to break away in order to have any chance of fulfilling my soul's destiny. I started making plans to move out and forward with my life. I had witnessed my mother-in-law's spirit ascend toward heaven, and I shared this breathtaking moment with my husband. His only response was a pat on the arm and a nod! I was totally excited but felt as though cold water had been thrown on me. I thought to myself, "Is that the best he can do?" **Goodbye control, I want to be me!**

§

CHAPTER 2

MIRACLES:
UNPLANNED
BUT DEFINITELY
DESIRED

ILLUMINATION

It was fate that we should meet, this beautiful romance was something that was meant to be, it didn't come by chance. I was guided down the path that led at last to you, and there I found my destiny and all my dreams come true.

--Unknown

To live alone a woman must establish credit, so this was my first planned task. I continued working a good job and applied for an American Express card. I borrowed $3,000 from the bank, held the money in a bank account, and didn't touch it. So when the loan was due, I was able to pay it back immediately. I never told anyone what I was doing, which wasn't difficult because my parents were in England. If they had even a hint that I was thinking about divorce, they would have been shocked because divorce was a sin to my family.

In 1981 my next plan of action was to start looking for an apartment. One night I had a very detailed dream about a new apartment's interior. I envisioned the colors and layout of the place and also saw it to be a town house. The following day, I stopped by an apartment locator's office during my lunch break, and the second town house he showed me was just like the one in my dream. The locator wanted to show me more apartments, but I knew this was the right one for me. I promptly paid a month's rent in advance, and during that month I went home everyday on lunch break and filled my car trunk to capacity to furnish the town house. I would put the car in the garage of my husband's and my house so the neighbors couldn't see what I was doing. I began the task of removing all of my personal items. I emptied my dresser and closet, and rearranged pictures and mirrors. Apparently, my husband didn't miss or notice any of these changes, as nothing was ever said. On the weekends I spent a lot of time cooking and packaging his favorite foods. After portioning and labeling, I stacked the foods in the freezer. There were enough homemade meals prepared for at least six months. Do know that I loved my husband, but I also understood that I could no longer live with him. Not only was he unwilling to grow spiritually, but he had no interest in supporting my own awakening and growth in this area.

I found many stock certificates in the closet with only my husband's name on them, so I guess he had his own agenda. I took with me the deed to land I had purchased with my own money several years earlier because it was clear there would be no more sharing in this relationship. At the time, however, I had no idea how important this land would be to my life in the future. I cleaned the house with a toothpick (literally), and then there was one last thing to do before I broke the news to my husband that I was leaving. I arranged for the movers to come and take the bedroom suite I had purchased that my husband didn't care about, plus a triple mirror he thought was "the ugliest thing" he had ever seen. (The mirror is actually every woman's dream and very beautiful.)

The night before I moved, I fixed dinner, bathed, and had my final suitcase ready to go. I waited until the evening news was over and even allowed my husband to take our two dogs for their usual walk. Then I broke it to him: "I want to tell you that at nine in the morning the movers are coming to take a few of my personal things because I am moving out." My husband went white, got up, and went to bed wordless. I slept on the sitting room floor and had the best night's rest. The following morning he left for work at 7:30, and not a word was spoken. At 9 o'clock the movers arrived, and that night I slept in my new town house. I was shaky but not fearful. (One of my cats was actually shakier than I.) In fact, I was excited about my new life and freeing myself to focus spiritually.

§

In the years that followed, I attended yoga classes diligently. Yoga is a discipline for life, and it takes awhile to adjust to the level of life changes involved. Yoga teaches that health and happiness originate within us, and no one can bring us peace but ourselves. This inner peace sustains while happiness from the outside is fleeting. Yoga began to change my vibration and subsequently, my life. I took endless meditation and healing classes of various kinds: iridology, massage, reflexology, hands-on healing, etc. I also met wonderful people who were on spiritual paths. I was never without a book and read works by Shirley MacLaine, Marianne Williamson, Louise Hay, Deepak Chopra, Leo Buscaglia, Wayne Dyer, Dean Ornish, Gary Zukav, Andrew Weil, Helen Steiner Rice, Sylvia Browne, and many more. I began fasting to cleanse my physical body starting at one day and then advancing up to 21-day periods. I had numerous colonics; went to a chiropractor; and began a series of rolfing sessions, which would last over 20 years. I had already incorporated natural healing in my diet for many years but began to do even more. I spent lots of money on nutrients and in the early '80s was one of the first customers to shop at the original Whole Foods grocery store in Texas. (The store reflected a movement to get back to the pure, natural basics of "whole" foods. It was a remarkable place then, and I knew it had a future; too bad I didn't invest in their stock at the time!) There is hardly a method I have not used to cleanse and heal my body and mind. In fact, because of the desire and passion to heal myself, I managed to lower my cholesterol by 20 points in one weekend while reading, studying, and letting go of harmful emotional baggage. It is truly incredible how blocked our bodies become as a result of our thinking.

Also at this time, I realized my passion for cats. My cat *Kitty* was withdrawn and unable to express herself other than backing into my face while I lay on my bed. I called her a closet cat because that's where she chose to live. Next door to my town house lived a gorgeous calico. The calico's owner had eight cats, and her boyfriend wasn't pleased because he didn't have a chair on which to sit. Fortunately, he made her put this beautiful calico outside, and that's when I met *Brandy*. Her fur was matted with mud and twigs, but I could see how special she was, and her owner said I could have her. Right away I took *Brandy* to my vet to get her bathed, groomed, shaved, and checked out. *Brandy* had intuition beyond description; thus began a major transformation in my life through this cat!

§

My ex-husband called me one day upset that he did not have any tenants for his rental house. I told him I would take the house, so just like that it became my new home. Ironically, I had remembered resenting his purchase of the house a couple of years before. At the time when I took occupancy, I was in the timeshare business and had at my disposal a team of service contractors; so I had the walls repainted, I had new carpet and linoleum installed, and I cleaned everything myself in great detail to make it like new.

Living alone and also without family during

holiday seasons, I chose to work at the Salvation Army at Thanksgiving and Christmas. Because my nature was that of a giver rather than a taker, I always gave back to the universe. Furthermore, I felt a bond with the people who had nothing, and I disliked both the greed and gluttony that often accompany the holiday season. I personally used these special days for fasting and for helping others, which was satisfying to my soul. I believe deep in our hearts we all know that when we die, what we *have* we will leave to others; what we *are* is ours forever. I had a *knowing* at a very early age – remember, my awakening began in the London theatre when I was climbing the stairs up to "The Gods" – that I wanted to *BE* the best me I knew how. I wanted to be sure I would get into heaven. I did not know how it would work out, but I always felt like I would do my part to make this world a better place for having been here. I knew I had discipline, my heart was open, I was strong in body and mind, and I was developing on a spiritual level. I was cleansing myself of past lives as well as this one. I was also open to receiving direction from God and learning to experience His love. However, this was not easy because I had never felt lasting love: not from my family (who were always squabbling) and not from my first marriage (because of so much criticism). My master teacher and life partner had not yet arrived to promote me, so the best was yet to come. Even though I was unaware of this, I was still willing to gain more clarity and longed to share my learning.

§

I soon had the new house arranged. I had **Brandy** and **Kitty**, and my divorce was settled.

Because I was finally free to go away and pursue my choices, I began to take weekend excursions, experiencing spiritual retreats and learning hands-on healing. I was so happy. I joined Unity Church and through the church met like-minded people such as Ritchie Mintz, a rolfer who has become a great friend. I was certainly on a different level of understanding my purpose in life as a result of all the classes I had taken and all the books I had read. Intuitive people let me know there was someone very special on the horizon, but it would be a year or two before I would meet this man (I was later told) – my partner of 14 lifetimes, my one true love. I kept working at whatever there was to do in order to grow. I felt like I was getting myself ready for this partner, as he was apparently preparing for me.

Life continued. On my birthday in 1982, it was a steaming 95 degrees. I was going to pick up a girlfriend, Rose Thompson, and head to the Riverwalk in San Antonio for the day. My mother had sent me $100 for my birthday, and I was planning to spend it to have a good time. That morning when I opened my garage door, a tiny orange kitten ran inside. He was so quick that it took me a minute to realize what I had seen. Having two cats already, I had canned food available and hastily set a plate for the kitten. I stayed a few minutes to be sure the little guy ate. He was eating, but I made a noise of some kind and he flew into the corner of the garage, or so I thought. I had boxes from my recent move stored and stacked there, and I assumed he was hiding behind them. I couldn't find him but needed to leave to meet Rose. I drove out of the garage very, very carefully. Rose and I stopped one time for gas on the 79-mile trip to San Antonio. As we slowed down at a stoplight, I heard and felt a strange noise under my car hood. I had told Rose about the incident with the kitten, so when she saw my face and heard my gasp at the sound, she said, "Oh, no, don't tell me what you're thinking."

I gingerly pulled the car over to a 7-11 store and opened the hood. You guessed it: there was the poor little kitten burning up from the heat of the road and the car. I asked Rose to run inside and get a cup of water. I retrieved the kitten, dabbed a tissue in the water to sprinkle on his mouth, and dipped his paws in the water. I could see clearly that his tail was damaged and bleeding, and I knew we had to find a vet. Unfortunately, it was Sunday at midday. Well, God moves in mysterious ways, and it took almost no time – as I was blindly driving down the roads without a map – to find an emergency vet, which appeared like a miracle out of the blue. To make a long story short, because the kitten's tail had gotten caught around a protrusion under the car hood, he managed to survive. However, his tail had to be amputated. It cost $100, the exact amount of money my mother had sent from London. Happy birthday to me! There was an empty shoebox in the trunk of my car, which is how we carried *Lucky* home. I then brought him to an empty room in my house where he was able to heal and where he lived for awhile.

Exactly one year later to the very day I had found *Lucky*, a rattlesnake bit him in my backyard. That morning, I saw *Lucky* lying limp on the concrete patio in a pool of blood, so I immediately took him to the vet. He spent three weeks in recovery at the vet hospital, and it was painful to watch him. I would visit him three times every day: before work, during my lunch break, and after work. I fed *Lucky* baby food on my finger and watched him gradually come back to a stage of strength where I could bring him home. It then took several weeks of daily bathing and covering *Lucky's* bare flesh with cream to heal his wounds because he had lost the fur on over 1/3 of his hindquarters. In the same bedroom where he had recovered from his tail amputation the year before, I laid clean sheets daily for *Lucky*, for he could not endure the fibers of the carpet on his flesh. I watched his body heal day by day. He made it and looked perfect again. I allowed him to walk around the house under my watchful eye, and he frequently went to the patio door wanting to go outside. Eventually one Sunday afternoon, I said a special prayer, opened the door, and let *Lucky* go outside. He went straight to the tree where my neighbors told me they had seen a rattlesnake (at my request, the tree hole was now filled with concrete), and he looked up at the tree like he was ready to take on that snake. *Lucky* lived 20 years with me as an outdoor cat and died of natural causes. Toward the end when he was sleeping on my fox fur stole, I believe I could see *Lucky's* love for me in his eyes. I certainly loved him and admired his strength and endurance.

§

In the early '80s, I responded to an ad for an assistant manager position at the new, still-under-construction WCT (World Championship Tennis) Resort in Lakeway, Texas. I distinctly remember the racket-shaped swimming pool being built the day I interviewed while I walked around wearing the required hard hat. I got the job working for the general manager, Jim Kane, who was my first big self-worth booster; it was also one of the most thrilling jobs of my life. I met Billie Jean King, Arthur Ashe, and many other top tennis stars and famous people. During the first big tournament at the resort, I had to work so many hours that I stayed overnight and on-call in a resort townhouse on site. One night, I was awakened from bed and called to the townhouse of Lamar Hunt, head of the Hunt Empire and owner of WCT. He had an urgent need to get out a press release, and I took the dictation. In those days a British secretary was a valued commodity; my shorthand and typing were fast and my organizational skills a gift, but I didn't really know it. I remember one day putting a training pamphlet on my boss' desk regarding a business class I wanted to take. He looked at me and said, "You could teach that class." No one had ever paid me such a compliment, and it was a life-altering, pivotal moment. I felt smart, capable, and worthwhile.

What happened to me later at WCT, however, would not be allowed today. Jim resigned, and I had to accept a new boss who was a cigarette smoker. Because cigarette smoke adversely affects my health, I burned candles all around the windowless office to diffuse the smoke. My boss did not care for this one bit. He also made sexual advances towards me and because I rejected him, he fired me during my seventh year with WCT. This would undoubtedly be cause for a lawsuit today.

My next job had a title, vice president, and involved much work with new experiences but little pay. I handled all of it with excitement and pride. I was beginning to understand my potential and talent as a manager of people, a trainer, an organizer, and a decorator. I had at least six timeshare resorts in various places for which I was responsible. I was happy with myself and traveled a great deal throughout the US, Mexico, and the Bahamas to do feasibility studies, decorating and furnishing timeshare resorts. I hired maids, managed staff, and trained them.

On my own time, I found astrologers, massage therapists, and healers everywhere I went. It was difficult trying to find tarot readers in places like Playa del Carmen, Mexico, when you don't speak Spanish; still, even in the middle of nowhere there was always an elder with wisdom to impart. Travels and searching for knowledge occupied my life for years, but I came home as often as possible to my indoor cats and many outside cats, which seemed to show up continuously. I also visited Houston to support my son in medical school. The timeshare company didn't last, however, and for whatever reason went kaput.

While in between jobs, I went to a Buddhist monastery in the northwestern mountains of Texas and lived with monks for a few days. I stayed on the side of a mountain in a shack with nothing, not even a door. I was strictly there to learn true meditation in an attempt to find myself. I attended services, obeyed the bells, and ate with the monks. Every few hours in the night the monks would ring these bells, which meant you had to get up, go to the chapel, stand, and chant until the last bell rang (a type of metaphysical discipline). Also during this time, I met a young woman in a neighboring shack who read my fortune by using rubles and tarot cards, and I was happy to hear that my future was bright! However, spiritual journey or not, after the third day I had had enough; I endured everything but realized it was all I could handle. I was not yet that evolved!

§

I lived alone with **Brandy**, **Kitty**, and **Lucky** for over a year, during which time I was without work. The economy wasn't good and even though my skills were the best, the market wanted someone younger. I was a perfectionist at housekeeping, so I always kept myself organized. Nothing appeared to be falling apart on the outside. But to quote Mother Teresa, "I know God will not give me anything I can't handle. I just wish that He didn't trust me so much."

At the time, I made frugal choices and went without heat and air conditioning, but the cats ate well. I had a very small portable heater and a 12-inch table fan; depending on the season, **Brandy** and I would sleep in the smallest room (the kitchen) on the floor because there was no suitable furniture on which to lie. I felt no deprivation, but sometimes it was hot! I like to think that I was building character during this eight-year period when I lived alone, studied, and learned that the path to enlightenment is not an easy one. Seldom was there instant gratification! I knew that rewards would come much later for me, perhaps in another lifetime. Even though my journey was a lonely one at this point, my soul was growing and I was joyful.

§

My next job was working for a chiropractor who became a wonderful role model for me. He was gifted, intuitive, and a healer; and he was *my* chiropractor, Dr. Mike Huneycutt. I've seen him

29

accept payments of homemade bread, cookies, and baskets of vegetables from those who couldn't afford monetary payments. How many doctors do that? I listened to every word Dr. Mike ever said to me and took advantage of every suggestion he made. He told me one time that he gave out crumbs, but I made loaves of bread from his direction. He was very influential in my life and will never know quite how much. He impressed me deeply and influenced my thinking in a lifelong beneficial way. In fact, Dr. Mike *changed my life*.

At this time, I found out more and more that cats were attracted to me. I had the three cats and many strays that kept showing up. I wore white clothing at the chiropractic job, and most people on the street thought I was a nurse or worked for a vet because of all the cats around my door. At any time of night or day, my neighbors would bring their sick cats and ask if I could help. I didn't mind. Again, life was good and I was happy with me. Still, there was something missing: a partner with whom to share my learning and my life.

§

In late May of 1988, I was working for an engineering company. I had spent an entire weekend analyzing my life and what I wanted. I went to work on a Monday morning and had a conversation in the office with a co-worker, a young lady named Theresa. She was like a daughter to me, there was a great amount of understanding between us, and I felt she admired me in spite of our age difference. (I was in my early 50s, and she was in her 20s.) I discussed my previous weekend and thoughts with her; I told Theresa that I wanted someone with whom to share my learning, to talk over the more expansive ideas I was enjoying, and who perhaps might be learning too. I always endeavored to spiritually embrace everyone; my arms and heart were open. I had read somewhere that if you write down in detail what you want in a partner, it will manifest. So several months before, I had written down the 100 things I had in mind. (Years after I met my man, I found out he was 90 plus of what I wanted, and much more.)

My boss was out of town, so Theresa and I were able to spend time talking. I told her I was seriously thinking about running a personal ad, but it was not supposed to be "cutesy." I also explained to her my desire to ask the universe if there was someone out there more interested in spiritual growth than the acquisition of material wealth. Theresa was like a teenager and said something to the effect of, "Oh yes, do it, do it." I said I would and before leaving the office for lunch, I told her, "I can tell you now what's going to happen: I'll either get a wheelbarrow full, or nothing." I then went home, called the newspaper, and read them my ad.

Very Special Lady – 5'2", 50+ wondering if there's a very special gentleman out there who's also choosing spiritual growth above acquisition of wealth and material things. Would love to share time and space if such gentleman exists. American-Statesman, Box W118, 78767

The lady in the classified section said, "Oh honey, that's lovely." So that day I had received two votes of confidence. I decided to run the ad for three days for the following Friday, Saturday, and Sunday (June 3-5). That was it, and now all I had to do was check the newspaper on Friday to be assured of the ad's appearance and then wait. I did a lot of thinking during this waiting period and wondered what I would do if I got any responses.

Theresa and I had talked all week, and on the following Monday she wanted me to go to the post office box to see if anything was there. I thought it was too soon since the ad had only been listed the previous Friday, so I waited until Tuesday to check. I could hardly believe it: the mailbox was full. My heart was racing when I got back to the office. My boss was still out of town, so I put the response letters I had received on my desk and said, "Theresa, help me." She was reluctant, thinking the letters were too personal. I quickly replied, "There's nothing personal here. Help me open them up." I can still hear Theresa's gasps as she opened the first one and said, "This is great. You have to read this right away." I was already reading a letter from a man who was sick. My compassionate heart told me to call the sick man before anyone else. Meanwhile, Theresa read aloud very dramatically a letter from a man named Jack Farley.

Dear Very Special Lady:

This represents a sincere reply to your ad in the personals column of the Austin American-Statesman. I believe that I may be the very special gentleman for whom you are searching. I am a single, white, 40-year-old male. I am 6'2" and weigh 185 pounds. I have blond hair and wear a full beard and glasses.

Now, a little about background. In May 1983, I divorced my wife of 17 years. We have one child from the marriage: a son who is now 19 and attending T.C.U in Fort Worth. Throughout the marriage, I struggled to climb the corporate ladder in the engineering business in Houston. Although I was quite successful, I felt that something was missing in my life. That "something" turned out to be spiritual direction.

After being helped in the right direction by some very loving friends, I became aware of a higher purpose in my life other than following other rats in the race. I quit the engineering business in June 1985 and began traveling. I first moved to Sedona, Arizona where I continued my spiritual awakening while earning a living as a home re-modeler. I next moved to Nevada near Lake Tahoe for the purpose of managing a New Age retreat and seminar center.

After one season at the seminar center, I moved to Oklahoma to help manage another Spiritual Community. It was there that I decided to pursue a career in writing, a career of which I have dreamed since childhood. I am currently living in Llano, where

I spend my time writing and remodeling a home for my parents.

I have recently finished my first major writing project: a book about my experiences in Vietnam. It is currently being circulated among several publishers. My current and future focus will center around writing about environmental issues, alternative health care, and spiritual growth.

As you can see, I have chosen to ignore the pursuit of fortune in deference to my pursuit of spiritual awareness and personal growth. I have never been happier than I am now; however, I miss the opportunity to share my happiness with a close companion.

I enjoy reading, bicycling, hiking, camping, and traveling. The type of traveling that I enjoy most is the type that is the least expensive and allows the most time to enjoy nature. I do not consider the distance between Llano and Austin to be a major obstacle in meeting and getting to know you. If you agree that we might be compatible, please give me a call.

Thank you for considering me as a partner in life.

Jack

I was gasping because I felt the letter was presumptuous and therefore controlling. I certainly wasn't going to call any control freak. Theresa and I opened all the letters that day, decided to which ones I would respond, and placed them in order of whom to contact. I might add that for days after this, I went to the newspaper box, and there were more and more responses.

That night I went home with my first stack of promising letters. The first gentleman I called was the one who was not feeling well. We had a good conversation but because he was under the weather, no plans were made. I ate my supper and for some reason my heart would race every time I picked up the letter from Jack Farley. If I remember correctly, it was close to 7:30 pm on Tuesday June 7, 1988 when I made the telephone call to Jack. I believe the phone only rang once and he said, "I knew it would be you, and I'll bet you have red hair." His words took my breath away. The next statement was, "I've been dreaming about you for years." I can hardly remember if I told Jack my name or not, but there was a magnetic connection. I told him about me, he told me about him, we talked about an hour, and I knew he was magic. (His voice was hypnotic and familiar.) Jack didn't know that I had a pile of phone calls to make, as I didn't tell him until later. He wanted to take me for dinner the next night and although I was not busy, I said I was. Being a Ms. Priss at the time, I was not going to be controlled in any way by someone else's expectations, so I said I would meet him in two nights at a downtown hotel, the Four Seasons. I did make a few more calls that night, but I was distracted by the power that Jack already had over me: the power of love!

In fact, Jack's actual physical response to my "Very Special Lady" ad was a remarkable miracle. On Friday morning, June 3, 1988 – the first of three days that my ad ran – while living in Llano, Texas,

Jack was remodeling his parents' retirement home. He had never read the Austin American-Statesman (which was also the major newspaper in Llano), but his parents had a subscription there, so when they visited to see the remodeling progress, they had a copy. For some reason, Jack was directed not only to read the June 3, 1988 Statesman, he was directed specifically to the personals column (an area he had never before perused). He opened the paper, turned to the personals page, ran his finger down the column, stopped on my ad, and said to himself, "There she is." He responded immediately, making use of his exceptional writing skills. Amazing.

On Thursday June 9 at 6:30 pm after a day of work, I made myself look my best and drove to our meeting place. I was right on time, not one minute early. I went through the door of the hotel, glanced around the room, and there he was: "my bearded wonder." As Jack unraveled himself from the chair in which he was sitting, I could see he was number one on the list of what I wanted in my man – he was very tall, and I loved the beard. I walked across the room and saw nothing but his eyes that had been described to me about a year before by a tarot reader, Hoortie Adamson. She told me that I would recognize my special man by his eyes because I had known him this way in many lifetimes. As I walked to Jack, I looked up and said, "Do you believe in hugs at first sight?" He said, "Absolutely," and he gave me the best hug I had ever had in my life, which literally swept me off my feet – the love, the warmth, the comfort, the strength, and everything I had ever wanted. Jack was big, but he was gentle; and his hands, though those of a laborer, were so soft. We had a soda in the lounge, and I felt nothing but his eyes penetrating my body and my every move. It was wonderful but quite frightening. (I learned later that it was pure love, something I had never experienced.) I didn't know that this particular evening Jack didn't have a penny to his name and that he had lost or given away his possessions to follow his heart humbly to God. (I found out later that Jack didn't even have a decent T-shirt to wear and had used his mother's credit card to buy one for our date. He was also sporting his only pair of shoes: old tennis sneakers.)

I didn't eat much because I was so nervous, and Jack was nervous too. We shared asparagus and then went for a walk along the lake. It was a warm evening, but Jack was perspiring profusely as if he was in the midday sun. I took a tissue, reached up, and mopped his brow. Jack then looked at me and said with intensity, "Get used to it," which took my breath away. I learned from him later that at that moment he knew he was going to marry me. I was everything that he had been dreaming of and looking for, but he still had hesitation about the big C, commitment. I was reluctant to pursue the relationship initially because of our age difference: Jack was 40, and I was 52.

This is how it began and it only got better. I did personally and graciously respond to every letter I received after I knew Jack was my choice, and I hoped that the right partner for each of these men was on the horizon.

§

As mentioned, Jack and I had our first meeting on Thursday June 9. We had our first real date on Saturday June 11. On Monday June 13, I received a greeting card – the first of many – in the mail from Jack:

> *"It seems as if I've loved you FOREVER. Maybe I have...*
>
> *Maybe we met in some other time where our lives touched this closely before. All I know for sure is this certainty inside me...*
>
> *...that we are meant for each other – NOW AND ALWAYS."*
>
> *I love you*
> *Jack*

§

Soon after we first met, Jack and I noticed that we would finish each other's sentences. I apparently had the same Oriental spirit guide as he in our dreams. Our thoughts were always in sync, and we laughed a lot about the familiarity we already had with each other. It's like we had no secrets, which is what we wanted. When I was told later that we had had 14 lifetimes of partnership, this level of familiarity was not surprising and we delighted in it. Our connection to each other was deep and intense. I never knew what love was until Jack and I met, and I never knew God – I only knew of God – until Jack's teachings.

On July 31, 1988, a month after I met Jack, I was reading my daily affirmations in the *Daily Word*, a publication from Unity (or Unity School). A particular excerpt was very touching to me, and I eagerly shared it with Jack (who, like me, had frequently attended Unity Church services). His excited response and our conversations discussing the affirmation cemented the bond that had already been strengthening. Jack's willingness to share the lesson from the *Daily Word* made me realize that our relationship undoubtedly had a promising future.

> *July 31, 1988*   *Sunday*
> *MY OWN GOOD COMES TO ME*
> *UNDER DIVINE LAW.*
> *IT CANNOT BE LOST OR*
> *WITHHELD FROM ME.*
>
> **Justice** *If we have any feelings of being unfairly treated, let us remember two important ideas: our own good comes to us under divine law; it cannot be lost or withheld from us. We do not have to fight for that which is our own under divine law, but we do have to be open and receptive to it. We have to claim it through faith and prayer. Let us set aside any thought that our good can be taken from us. Such thoughts only limit us and keep us in an anxious, negative state of mind. We do not want to cling to things that really are not our own, things that we have no need of now. The good that God has for us is a flowing, growing good. It is keyed to our present needs, our present place in thought, and consciousness.*
> *"Great and wonderful are thy deeds...!*
> *Just and true are thy ways." --Rev. 15:3*

§

Jack had lost everything in the stock market crash of the '80s: houses, cars, money, and his wife. He then began his spiritual journey, earning his daily bread at various retreats in Sedona, Arizona and elsewhere. Right before Jack entered my life, he had spent several months releasing his pain from the Vietnam War by writing a book called *Little Victories*. He had offers to publish it but was requested to change the tense in order to diminish the facts so the book wouldn't sound autobiographical and critical. Jack didn't budge and kept the book exactly as he had written it. *Little Victories* is a truly fascinating account of what Jack experienced on a mission – which was secret, something he never mentioned to me – in Cambodia while designing and building bridges. (He received numerous commendations and medals from the US Navy for his efforts.) I really admire the honesty in Jack's writing and his resolve not to change the facts, and I am anxious to get the book published myself to benefit our animal refuge.

§

At the time I met Jack, he was using his engineering and general contractor skills in Llano to remodel the aforementioned retirement home for his parents. His parents were living in Houston at the time, and his father had recently been diagnosed with cancer. Jack was doing an incredibly good job of expanding and remodeling the house, and with my innate decorating skills I was able to help him. His parents did come to Llano and lived there for almost a year, during which time Jack worked their land, which had not been farmed in years. He developed this land and produced what we were told was the biggest organic garden in the state of Texas at that time. Jack sold the produce to Whole Foods and other natural food stores in Austin, San Antonio, and small towns in between.

Jack and I also formed a small business: TLC (Tender Loving Care) Partners. He loved cats and built cat furniture, and we went to craft shows to sell the products. It was a brand new thing at the time. The kitty condos were carpeted like you see them in commercial pet stores nowadays. At one of the craft shows in Round Rock, Texas, the Society for the Prevention of Cruelty to Animals brought in cats and dogs for adoption, and I noticed a beautiful lab cocker mix with red golden hair (the exact shade of my own!). The moment I saw him, I told Jack, "That is my dog." I said, "If that dog doesn't find a home by the end of the day, then he comes home with us." Well, he did come home with us, and we named him *Pardy*, short for partner. *Pardy* was the most loyal, protective, and loving dog anyone could wish for. I'm not sure how old he was when we first adopted him, but he lived with us over 13 years.

For almost a year, Jack and I endured a long-distance relationship between Austin and Llano. Of course, 50 miles is not that long of a distance, but there were times when it was tiring. Love can have you do difficult things sometimes.

Around this time, Jack suggested we take a weekend spiritual retreat in northeast Texas. At the end of the weekend we were given a form on which to write our life goals. Everything I wrote and dreamed about – in Jesus' name – would come true in the coming years.

§

Seven months after I met Jack, his father passed away. Although Jack had a brother and a sister, there wasn't very much support from either one for the caring of his father, and subsequently his mother. This, of course, was his family's business, and at the time I didn't understand it. I knew that Jack promised his mother he would stay with her and help her as long as he could. She – like my mother with me – had control over him, and I saw this clearly. I truly loved Jack, and if all I ever had from him or with him was a little weekend time, then I felt I could live with that. I said nothing; all I did was think, "Oh my goodness, if he could just say no to his mother." One week after those thoughts, Jack called me and said, "I need you to help me leave my mother."

I had my own house, but I am from the old school and didn't want my man moving into my space without some form of commitment. I let Jack know this, so he asked me to marry him. We didn't have money; we just had each other. So we planned a spiritual union with God as our only witness. Jack had recently taken *Pardy* to Sedona with a load of kitty condos for sale following a circuit of craft shows. He stayed with a friend of mine, Datha Farrington – a spiritual therapist and astrologer – in Oklahoma City. Jack also stayed in Glendale, Arizona with another friend, Audrey Hunt – a talented intuitive. He made this entire journey an opportunity for free thinking and decision making. While he was gone, I prepared my house for his arrival and "move in."

I didn't see Jack again until the day of our first "commitment ceremony," which was at the Horseshoe Bay Chapel overlooking the lake in Marble Falls, Texas. We paid $25 to have the chapel to ourselves. It was magnificent. Angels were there, God was there, and Jack was there sweating profusely. I was giggling like a schoolgirl. We read each other the vows we had written.

FIRST WEDDING
Jack's VOWS of November 14, 1989
God As Our Only Witness

WITH THIS RING, which is the
symbol of our holy oneness,
I PROMISE to you,
DOROTHY ANN ROSE, all my Love
from all lifetimes brought into and
intensified at this moment;
I PROMISE to honor your holiness and
always recognize the Goddess within you;
I PROMISE to support you in attaining the most
holy presence to which you aspire;
I PROMISE to be by your side and accompany
you through all healing, knowing that as
you heal, so too do I;
I PROMISE to walk with you in
Grace and seek only truth;
I PROMISE to seek with you the
world beyond this;
I PROMISE to give all that I have to you.
Knowing that as I do, I am giving to myself;
I PROMISE to help you determine what
of this world holds value for you;
I PROMISE to honor your wishes as to
the physical supports you may desire;
AND, I PROMISE to be your
Masterful Companion for the
remainder of this time on earth.
Jack

Jack's vows were so intensely profound that they frightened me at the time because I felt a level of control from them. I learned much later that this was far from their meaning. Jack spoke of the love from many lifetimes in which we had been together, intensified at that one moment in the chapel at Horseshoe Bay. He KNEW of this level of love; I did not.

Our wedding cake was one cheesecake cupcake with one candle along with a mini-bottle of champagne, both of which we shared and very much enjoyed. The sun was shining brightly as we sat on the Horseshoe Bay grounds, and the temperature was 85 degrees. It was simply a wonderful day, and we spent that night at a very small cabin in the hills of Texas. I remember looking down from the balcony at the scenery of the hills as the sun set. I knew I had the whole world in my hands and was so glad to be me. The next day we enjoyed the morning strolling through the town of Wimberley – a small art center and spiritual space – while window-shopping at antique and craft stores. We then drove to "our" home.

§

The economy was not good at this time. Jack decided to make a journey to San Francisco, where there had recently been a serious earthquake, to see if he could get engineering and building work. The thought of separation from Jack was most painful, so I traveled behind his camper in my car in order to spend the first night away from home with him. The next morning I returned to Austin, and Jack headed west. We did not have cell phones in those days, but both of us had tape recorders; so as soon as we parted, we began taping our thoughts and emotions, which we mailed to each other daily.

Within 48 hours of Jack's arrival in the San Francisco area, he told me he could not endure the hectic energy and was planning to try Lake Havasu, Arizona. He worked in Lake Havasu for about nine months and lived out of his camper. Jack flew back home after four and a half months of being apart, and we were both deeply heartbroken when he had to return to Lake Havasu for more work. Jack had not had his own home in years, so we planned that he would come back permanently in September. Upon his return, Jack's confidence had strengthened, so we decided to form Heart Construction Company. Our motto was, "Our heart is in our business." It certainly was in everything we did. (We had all of $7,000 but felt like the richest people on earth.) With our togetherness in spirit, we knew we were on the right track and could do no wrong. The business started slowly, but as the years went by – because of Jack's impeccable reputation, skills as an engineer/architect, and inherited gift (from his grandfather) of carpentry – the work increased and it was a joy ride.

Soon after Jack's return in September, I did what Hoortie Adamson suggested I do: show Jack some land that I owned. She had said about Jack, "Oh honey, he's going to build you your dream house," even though I never knew I had a dream house in mind. I had owned the land since 1971, and it had not been touched in 18 years. Jack and I took a Sunday afternoon to explore it, and he brought an old machete so we could hack our way through the brush. We didn't know where we were on the land, but we knew this was the place we wanted to live. It was "our" place, and we felt it.

45

As I've said, I never knew what love was until I met Jack. Jack was love. He was extraordinarily gifted in so many ways but especially at directing meditations. Jack would spiritually remove us from our bodies, elevate us, and take us from our living room to the land, where we would hover – suspended in the air – over our envisioned home. And at sunrise on Sundays, we would drive to the land, find the same little spot each time with the same little rock and the sun shining through the trees, and lie on the ground in each other's arms. Jack would take us on other meditations while on the land; and as far as we were concerned, we were already living in our new house. Let it be understood that we had little money, and I still had a small mortgage on the house in which we were living. So we didn't know how or when this was going to happen; we just KNEW it would.

One year later we were making a moderate salary and wanted to make our marriage a legal one. Marriage "before God" is good, but on this earth plane, making it legal is essential. So we decided to do just that. I found a perfect wedding gown, we bought Jack the perfect suit, we applied for and obtained the legal marriage license, and we established the date for November 14, 1991. This was exactly two years after our first spiritual union. An ordained minister friend performed the legal union, and another friend of 30 years was our only witness. We married in a wedding chapel so that the music and environment were official, and this time our wedding cake was a little larger. The weather did not cooperate, for it was considerably cooler than our first union and drizzle was in the air.

It didn't matter, though – I was Jack's lady and he was my man. We chose this song:

> *I am your lady and you are my man. Whenever you reach for me I'll do all that I can.*
> *We are headed for somewhere. Somewhere we've never been. And although we are frightened, we are ready for the power of love.*

Jack had also come across two symbolic name cards on his travels to New England, and we found them to be very appropriate for this special day:

Jack "Successor"	Dorothy "Gift of God"
See what love The Father Has bestowed Upon us That we should Be called Children of God. I John 3:1	*Trust in the Lord with all your heart and lean not on your own understanding.* Proverbs 3:5

After the ceremony, Jack and I went home to have our second honeymoon. My bearded wonder gallantly carried me over the threshold and then promptly excused himself to the bathroom. The champagne, rich wedding cake, and excitement were just too much for him!

We lived very happily, loving our life and appreciating everything. Business improved with more referrals and bigger jobs, so we bought newer vehicles and remodeled and repaired the house in which we were living. Still, we wanted to build the house of our dreams. I owned the land but in order to get a loan to build the new house, the bank insisted that we appoint a builder even though Jack could have done everything alone. (He had helped design and develop cities in Texas, for example!) We found a builder through a friend and were then able to get started. Applying for a loan and having to sell the house we occupied in order to qualify for the loan was a whirlwind of activity with Jack working full-time with my assistance; nevertheless, where there is a will, there is a way.

In between Thanksgiving and Christmas in the cold winter of 1993, Jack rented earthmoving equipment and cleared the land himself. He then built a magnificent winding driveway from the street to where the house would be and constructed a huge lumber storage building for Heart Construction. We had to hire help for mulching the cedar brush, which was a humongous task. We marked the sides of the 350-foot driveway with tape to protect construction equipment from damaging the trees we were keeping and protecting. Jack dug and laid the drive basecoat ready for asphalt. We then hired more men to professionally remove the enormous cedar stumps and haul them off site. Everything was being prepared, and everything was secured with signage to protect existing wildlife. Jack and I handled all we did with great care and respect for the land and wildlife. We loved this place and felt the sacredness of God's space. We found flint stones among the thousands of piled rocks where we determined the house would be, and we thought perhaps this rock formation indicated that the land was once an Indian burial ground. The sacredness was not definable but was very much felt and honored.

Late afternoon on New Years Eve 1993, the loan was approved, and we signed the papers as the last customers of the year. What a gift and a good beginning for the New Year! That night I sang to Jack an old British song:

> *With someone like you, a pal good and true, I would like to leave it all behind and go and find a place that's known to God alone, a perfect spot to call our very own. We will find perfect peace where joys never cease, somewhere beneath a sunny sky. We will build a sweet little nest, somewhere in the west, and let the rest of the world go by.*

And so began the building in January 1994 of our "sweet little nest," which was completed on April 16, 1994. We, especially Jack, had done so much of the work and were both very proud of finishing construction so quickly. Our old house was sold in a timely manner. We then moved most of our furniture by ourselves in Jack's truck and my van and had movers bring the larger pieces. On April 16 we spent the first night in our new love nest. Jack built our offices, his workshop, and our front gate with my assistance; we were always a team and worked so well together! Jack had talked me into leaving the insurance company I was working for to help him on job sites to clean up, lay tile, etc. Helping and spending time with Jack was fun for me. He taught me so much; and as he said in the beginning, my working with him saved him more money than the small salary I earned. Many people I knew and worked with said that Jack and I being together day and night wouldn't work. How wrong they were! When two or more people come together with God, there is nothing that can't be done.

At that time, we had three dogs: **Pardy**, **Tyke** (a German Shepherd I had found as a puppy roaming the streets), and **Lovey** (a three-legged border collie I had found in a local park at 6 am one day). Jack built appropriate kennels and everyone got along well.

Then there were the cats. The weekend before we moved into our new house, Jack took a few days to build the first "Cat House." This is a dear little building with shelving and windows adequate enough to handle the four house cats I was already caring for: **Brandy**, **Queeny**, **Kitty**, and **Lucky**. I hate to say it, but as much as I loved cats, I didn't want their fur on my new house carpet, at least not at that time. I started with a sign for *Cat House* and have since put signs on every building we have constructed: from *The Park* to *The Manger* where we house hay, to *The Well* and *Trough I* and *Trough II* where we feed the deer. Because only two of the six acres of this land are cultivated, if you have no reference point, you can easily get lost.

Two nights before we moved into the new house and were still living at the old one, I came as usual to the land to check on, feed, and give some love to the cats and dogs. (Typically, I would do this two or three times a day.) This particular night I noticed that **Kitty** was behaving strangely, going in circles outside *Cat House*. I didn't really know then, but now after 10 years of experience of having over 100 cats, I know that **Kitty** was probably having or had had a stroke. I spent over an hour with **Kitty** holding her, petting her, loving her, talking to her, and crying with her, as I sensed that this might be one of our last times together. I placed her in a soft, low, comfortable bed inside *Cat House* and left with a deep sadness in my heart. We had a trap door so the cats could go out, but at night we locked the "in" portion so no night creatures could venture inside. The next morning, I assumed that *Kitty* had gone out, and I never saw her again although we combed the property. About three or four weeks after we had moved into the house, our next door neighbor introduced himself and asked if we had perhaps lost a little gray cat. He had seen her body a few weeks earlier on our property along his fence line but when we looked, she of course was gone. I knew *Kitty* was wearing a collar, but I never found it. At least I knew that she had transitioned in her own time and safe space. I have continuously blamed myself for leaving the trap door "out" portion open, and it's been closed ever since this heart wrenching experience. In fact, I have subsequently made every effort to make sure that all the cats are safely locked in their buildings every night. All buildings have extended, attached runs that are totally secure so the cats don't have restrictions, but they have protected limitations. *Kitty's* departure was the first of many that we have had here, and every time a cat dies my heart breaks into a million pieces. When I find their precious bodies, I have them cremated at the Rainbow Bridge Pet Crematory in Manchaca, Texas. Butch Garza, the owner and operator, has been very kind and helpful to me.

Jack and I became aware very soon after moving in that there were several herds of deer roaming the land, and we also learned – since we are both city folk – that deer follow the same trails for hundreds of years. We began to study these trails on our land, and we saw where the deer entered and where they exited to cross the street to other peoples' land; it is essentially a circular trip. When Jack and I saw this pattern, we realized where we would build troughs for the corn and seed mix, a manger for the hay, and water pan tables. Originally, we had six or seven feeding stations, but for Jack the distance of 700 to 800 feet of carrying several hundred pounds of corn every week became too much. He was already pretty worn out by the end of the week after building and hauling lumber for five days for Heart Construction, so we consolidated the land feeders. It still takes me 45 minutes to an hour every other day to fill the wildlife water pans. I put out corn and seed daily and do it joyfully, but it is time consuming and I need help hauling the 50-pound bags of corn and seed to the storage barrels each week.

§

Our *Brandy* was the most precious calico cat. She lived a protected and happy life, and she gave direction and purpose to both Jack and me. I shall never forget *Brandy's* sweetness and comfort during the seven-year down period when I lived alone before I met my beloved. *Brandy* was so intuitive; she kept my secrets, endured my tears, and had more love in her paws than many people have in their whole being. *Brandy* showed compassion and was always there when my first tears fell in what I thought was silent seclusion (in fact, she would come running from the other end of the house); she knew, she heard, and she was there! *Brandy* was a true best friend, and her heart was huge. She lived with me for at least 13 years and transitioned after one year at our new home with grace and dignity after a severe illness. ***Brandy*** showed Jack and me her best face just hours before taking off to places selected and known only to her, for we never found her precious body. Friends who are far more evolved than I tell me that ***Brandy*** wanted us to remember her looking her best, so she put on a show, and it worked.

Recognizing "Our Mission" was the pure joy of ***Brandy's*** memory. Yes, a small calico cat can so impress your heart and life as to give it meaning and purpose. In my estimation, ***Brandy*** was sent from God to open our hearts to the deepest level where we would feel and see things we never understood. Thus, Jack and I dedicated our lives – Our Mission – to nurturing feral, unwanted, undernourished, and damaged homeless cats. We knew we couldn't save them all, but we could darn sure try! We rescued without harm, returned to abundant health, loved, and cared for these little people in cat suits in a safe, protected environment. We promised God that we would care for any cat that came to our land; and in between, we would adopt two or three cats from the Humane Society, Paws, or other similar agency at Christmastime as gifts to each other. Jack and I always selected the cats no one else wanted – the supposedly not-so-cute ones (to us, they are all beautiful) – and we frequently rescued them the night before they were to be put to sleep. Jack and I gave in all ways to accomplish this: Our Mission, our purpose, and our bliss. And it is now "My" Mission to fulfill and complete, and I am truly thankful to help make the world a better place.

§

For how many years do we humans ask the question, "Why am I here?" For how many years do we not see that the simple thing we are doing is both our passion and exactly why we are here? It may not have anything to do with earning money, and it certainly may not have us in the public eye; however, we all have our own special mission or purpose in life. In some way, our purpose is our gift to the universe that makes this world a better place. Frequently this involves hard work, yet we get lost in the passion of doing the work and forget ourselves. Jack worked full-time to earn a living that supported our commitment. My work is 365 days a year, but that is okay with me. My salary is not in the form of a weekly check but rather in the satisfaction of a job well done. By the end of each week, 175 potty boxes have been cleaned, 63 buildings disinfected, and clean linen/blankets put on beds for 58 cats. Also, 300 pounds of dry food are unloaded and distributed weekly, as are 12 cases of sorted canned food. There are nine buildings, and presently I am finishing Our Mission with the cats in Jack's memory. There is always much to be done. I honor God's beautiful creatures, and I honor the man whose idea it was to create this space.

In addition to this work with cats, Jack also would buy, load, and unload tons (literally) of corn and seed for other wildlife (mostly deer, birds, and foxes). He then distributed this to both our *Feed Depot* storage building and feed barrels we have around the property. For this place is a National Wildlife Federation Backyard Wildlife Habitat called **CAT HAVEN**. Without Jack's physical presence now, young men help me with his work.

I continue to mix our own quality of birdseed. Salt and mineral blocks are dispensed for the deer, and clean hay is laid on the hillside to keep them from slipping on the slopes. Wood shavings – on which the deer can rest and give birth without being disturbed – are scattered in selected spaces in the spring, as are 75 bags of cypress mulch for repairing the deer trails around the property paths. Because the deer have walked these trails for hundreds of years, it would truly be unfair to change their route; so it is important to follow their paths closely to fulfill their needs.

§

CAT HAVEN, resort for cats, was constructed in 1996. *Brandy* had transitioned in 1995 and it so devastated me, mostly because I could not find her beautiful body. My mind, energy, and spirit were deeply hurt. Obviously recognizing my pain, Jack said, "Okay, let's do something in *Brandy's* memory." Well, that was the beginning of the awakening. Jack then said, "Because you like cats so much, let's build a building where you can house them. You decide what it is you want, and I'll build it." So I set about researching through town to see what the best boarding facilities were like. I found the so-called "best," but I knew Jack and I could create a better boarding home. I designed and Jack constructed a deluxe building with huge floor-to-ceiling spaces and pure white walls, lots of shelves on which the cats could climb, cedar posts on which they could scratch, and two windows per space for them to look outside. Everything was white (purity), pink (personal love), and green (healing); thus, we built a *loving* and *healing* center for cat boarding.

I knew when I began my spiritual adventure many years before, that someday I would have my own healing center; I just never knew it would be for animals. Jack and I designed business cards with *Brandy's* picture and flyers stating the desirability of this place: peaceful, in the woods, owners on-site and on duty 24 hours. We did quite well for awhile, but I soon realized that I did not enjoy dealing with people. I loved the cats, but that was about it. So Jack and I gave up boarding.

The building was empty for over a year, and from time to time Jack and I would go inside, look at this magnificent creation, sigh, and ask God, "What do you want us to do with this?" At the time I was caring for the three dogs, all strays that I had found on the highway. I used to walk them every morning about 6:00 in a local park (or rather they walked me, because *Tyke* was 85 pounds and I'm only 105). One morning, I heard a strange sound in the park brush and found a sable gray cat. Fortunately, she was agreeable enough for me to carry her to the car with three dogs barking at my heels, get her in the car, and drive home safely without a major catastrophe. But I was wondering the whole time what to do with this cat. Then it occurred to me that I had a 30-foot-long building with accommodations for 28 cats! Obviously, this was plenty of room to comfortably house the new cat, whom we appropriately named *Sable*. Thus began the process of realizing I was not supposed to board cats and expect payment, but rather take cats into a loving environment and provide for them forever.

The *Cat Haven* building was the beginning of the ideal place to care for the cats; bond with them; have them heal from neutering, spaying, or any ailments; play with other cats; and very soon be part of our family. It seemed that every week while walking in this same park, another pitiful looking cat would appear in the long grass or behind a bush, and somehow I would get him/her to my car despite the dogs. I finally put a cat carrier inside the vehicle to accommodate what seemed to be a destined series of events. A few of the rescued cats were in very bad condition but with exception of one who was diagnosed with AIDS, every story had a happy ending. Jack and I figured that these cats were either dumped in the park or strayed of their own accord. *Sable* was with us for almost three years and would always volunteer to mother new kittens we rescued. When *Sable* left us, Jack and I could not understand why because she was so loved and so loving in return. (We realized later that we hadn't adopted any new kittens this particular year, so there weren't any for *Sable* to mother. That may be why she left us.) Through our tears we found the peace of letting *Sable* go, even though we missed her and cherished the one or two pictures we had of her. Allowing the cats to choose (which building they want to live in, friend selection, etc.) has been a major lesson and all part of understanding their needs to express themselves and be happy.

In the beginning **CAT HAVEN** was the only building in which to place new family members. (There was *Cat House*, but my four older cats already occupied it.) Initially when we first rescued a cat, Jack and I would take the lovely animal to **CAT HAVEN**, secure the cat in a personal eight-foot-high shelved cubical with two windows, allow the cat to heal, and let him/her bond with us through daily handling and routine reliable times of feeding special canned foods. (Dry food and water is always available.) After a couple of months, we would let the cat loose in the building to bond with other cats. Jack later added the *Patio Garden* – a 10-foot extension to the back of **CAT HAVEN** – which allowed the cats to go in and out through a trap door to a securely screened section with a roof so that they could get a safe feel for the outdoors while getting prepared to actually go outside.

It was always a special event to let a cat outside the building and onto the land for the first time after recuperation. While paying very close attention, Jack and I allowed the cats out during the day for an hour or so at first and then longer, as they would become less fearful and more aware of the comforts inside the buildings. We put the cats inside at night to protect them from wildlife, and they soon became accustomed to the clock, waiting for us at the door or window ready to play outside. Soon after the *Patio Garden* addition, we added the *Annex*, yet another extension of the outside effect, which is actually a hidey-hole space for cats who want to be alone. In 2006 Jack added a covered outside run. In sum, there are 10 cat buildings. *Cat Haven* stands alone; the other buildings – *Cat House, Pardy's Pen, Bunk House, Barracks, Playhouse, Ruffhouse, Sick Bay, Feed Depot,* and *Playroom* – are known as **The Village at CAT HAVEN**.

With so many cats, it is paramount to have a great veterinarian, and I'm happy to say that I have the best: Dr. Ron Stried. He is a very supportive, accommodating, and gifted doctor who not only treats my animals with love and care, but treats me the same way, especially when my "babies" have to be put down. I parted with five cats and *Pardy* in one year, and Dr. Stried was more than comforting during that time. Also, all of my cats are microchipped, and Dr. Stried gave me a very fair deal on this procedure. He even sent a vet tech to the property to have this done so the cats could stay in the comfort of their own homes. To me, Dr. Stried is a miracle worker.

§

Jack and I continued our life with bountiful work and also had miraculous vacations. The years with Jack were positively wonderful. Our worldwide travels consisted of trips to London to meet my parents and my British friends of over 60 years. Jack made three trips to London; I made four, one being a daughterly duty trip to help my folks. We spent several weeks on the Isle of Wight (not primitive by any means but definitely old England with quaint pubs serving steak and kidney pie, fish and chips, and other typically English fare), visited Sir Alfred Lord Tennyson's home there, and spent many hours walking up to the monument built in Tennyson's honor. On two consecutive visits to the island, I experienced a past life where sadness brought me to my knees. I could feel myself waving goodbye to a ship and sensed most definitely that it was Jack aboard the ship and that we were saying sweet but painful farewells. It happened at the same place in two consecutive years when I put my foot on a certain spot on the island. There are no words to describe it; I just buckled from the sense of the loss and felt distinctly like it was the loss of my love, Jack.

On our three trips to England together, Jack and I always visited the Isle of Wight first to recoup for a week. Then we would go to London and thus enter the realm of my mother's control. My dad was easy; he just wanted to sit and talk, which we did. But we also did the entire London sightseeing trip – Buckingham Palace, the Tower of London, St. Paul's Cathedral, Westminster Abbey, all the parks, and The Strand Theatre. On the second London trip, Jack and I rented a limousine for my mother's 80th birthday (my father was close to 90 at the time), took my parents to Claridges for tea, and then took them around London in the limo to see the new developments since they were no longer able to get around themselves. We had a good time on all three trips because Jack and I were together. My parents really liked Jack, and he was so willing to help. He hauled huge floor mats to the laundry and washed everything (curtains, bedspreads, etc.) while I cleaned the house and re-hung the draperies. Their flatlet was spotless when we left.

The fourth trip was different because I was going for two weeks alone to take care of paper work and business matters for my parents. As an only child, this appeared to be the daughterly thing to do. It was so hard on me just thinking about leaving Jack. I was not a happy girl, and I could sense Jack's apprehension days before I left. We got to the local airport where I was a basket case and couldn't stop crying. In those days you could buy a ticket at the airport, and I asked if Jack would come at least to Dallas with me, which he did. This helped because it meant we were together for another four hours before I crossed the Atlantic. I cried during most of the journey to England, I couldn't eat, and I know I irritated the man next to me. It was a difficult two weeks during which I felt choked and stifled by my overly attentive parents; but I made it, and my returning was jubilant. Jack was at the airport to greet me with smiles and flowers. I vowed I would never leave him again for anything or anyone.

§

Because Jack and I liked to travel but were solely responsible for 60-plus cats and a wildlife refuge, we needed to hire someone to care for the cats and wildlife while we were away. I had everything super organized, and our employee, Kristina, would come everyday to clean, change the cats' boxes, check their food and water, and give them love. Jack and I were thus able to travel the world and the US; especially important was Santa Fe, where he had written *Little Victories*. (Jack showed me the concrete bench by his campsite where he had written this incredible book; I was moved, to say the least. Jack took a beautiful photo of the bench with the sun's rays shining through the trees onto it.) On our US journeys we would always take **Pardy**, a great traveler who loved to be in the backseat of the pickup truck. He loved the snow in the mountains and to sleep in the truck and guard it when we wanted to shop.

A water sports enthusiast, Jack loved to dive, snorkel, and whitewater raft; the reward of planned trips – many of which involved these water sports – motivated him to work intensely every year. Jack and I believed that while hard work is essential, so is fun and travel. We cruised round trip to Hawaii; went through the Panama Canal three times; traveled to Honduras, Fantasy Island, and Belize on multiple occasions; and several times went to Costa Rica, which has some of the best whitewater rafting in the world. I will point out that I am highly allergic to sulfur and got quite sick due to a reaction from the volcanic eruptions while touring the Hawaiian Islands. So our trips weren't always perfect! But with Jack, travel was always first class or not at all. We had the most expensive suites aboard ships and lived in total luxury when on the road.

On one of our vacations to Belize and the Mayan ruins, we had a delightful guide. We let him know that we were interested in anything new he had to show us, so he took us for a little walk deeper into the rain forest. Then quite suddenly, the guide went to Jack's side, pulled down an enormous branch from a palm tree, held it in front of both of us, and said: "There, now you are married again." Jack and I laughed and asked the guide to please take a photograph. We figured we were now married three times!

§

One day out of the blue Jack asked me if there was anything else he could do to make my life happier. I responded immediately, "Learn to dance," and he did. Neither one of us thought Jack had rhythm, so it was a big surprise when we realized he could dance. We took over a year of private lessons and practiced a lot, soon recognizing that for every hour of concentrated instruction there had to be 7 to 10 hours of practice. We learned 16 dances, but there were 6 or 7 that we liked the most because we were the best at them: the Latin dances and rock-and-roll swing dances. Jack and I became quite good considering our height difference, we frequently got applause, and most nights we received many compliments on our skills. People watched our feet because in real ballroom dancing, the foot patterns and posture are what count (not so much the body gestures). Dancing truly enhanced our lives; we were like school children, and Jack would follow the band venues to decide where we would go two or three nights each week. We became friends with band members and their wives, both of us lost weight, and it was absolutely pure fun.

§

King was a cat who came into my life three weeks after *Queeny* died. What follows a queen but a king? *King* was jet black except for one tiny spot under his chin. I found him in the woods by a barbecue restaurant. When I first entered the restaurant to pick up my order, *King* came up to me from under a bush. I leaned over and right away petted him. He had no fear, but I could see from his eyes and his nose that he either had an allergy or some sort of weakness. I went inside and asked the owner if this was his cat. He said no, and I then asked him if he knew to whom the cat belonged. The response was, "He just lives outside." When I looked outside and saw that there was nothing habitable for a cat, I picked up this precious creature, carried him home in my van, and put him in *Cat House* with *Kitty* and *Brandy*. I took our *King* to the vet the next day, and apparently he had a bronchial problem and was in need of medication right immediately. Otherwise, *King* was healthy with an exceptionally fine, unique disposition. Jack and I called him the greeting ambassador to **CAT HAVEN** because he welcomed every new cat who showed up on the property. *King* never hissed at or struck another cat and became very vibrant after several weeks of recuperation in and adjustment to his new home. He seemed to be an ideal house

63

cat, so he moved from *Cat House* to our house. *King* went from living in a drainage ditch under a barbecue restaurant to sleeping on a fox fur stole. Not bad!

About a year after I found *King*, there were some little girls outside PetSmart giving away kittens. The last kitten they had was a calico, and I immediately thought of *Brandy*. When I saw this kitten, I said to myself, "Oh my gosh, maybe this is *Brandy* reincarnated." I told the little girls that if I came out of the store and they still had her, I would take her. Of course, this is what happened, and now *King* had a girlfriend named *Callie*. In the beginning, they were very close, becoming bosom buddies. *Callie* was only five or six weeks old and *King*, according to the vet, was two to three years of age.

King lived joyfully and graciously for over 10 years as the ambassador for **CAT HAVEN**. One night in 2006, Jack and I came home from a very happy evening of dancing and found our little *King-King* limping around in a circle. We could tell that he had lost the use of one his legs, so we picked him up and sat on the couch together, kissing and snuggling him before we took him to an emergency center. The vet technicians immediately put *King* in an isolation chamber of pure oxygen and said he wouldn't make it through the night without this. It was already 2 or 3 am when Jack and I went home to change and see if we could get some sleep; I, of course, could not.

Jack had an appointment with a customer on this Saturday morning, so I went to the emergency center to check on *King*. He was still alive, but I don't think he recognized me. The vet techs put the oxygen chamber and oxygen canister in my car, and I took *King* to Dr. Stried. Unfortunately, we had to put *King* to sleep. As I always do for my animals, I prepared *King's* favorite soft bed and blanket to cover him. I had flowers, toys, and notes of love to show how much he meant to us. *King* was cremated at Rainbow Bridge Pet Crematory. They put his ashes in a beautiful cedar chest, which I then placed on his favorite chair in the house (where they are to this day). I also put *King's* bell collar on the cedar chest with *Callie's* picture by its side. (On occasion, I still pick up the cedar chest with the bell collar, sit on the couch with it, and *Callie* comes running at the sound of the bell to sit beside me.) Jack and I were sad for days, sorely missing *King's* presence in the house.

Twelve days after *King's* transition, Jack told me on this particular morning that he needed help loading something into his truck at the gate. This was an unusual occurrence because Jack and I typically said goodbye at the house. While I was carefully closing the gate after Jack left, I noticed at eye level an enormous butterfly/moth on the gate. It was thick and fat, was heavily dusted with yellow-brown pollen, and had a wingspan of about five inches. Its most striking feature, however, was in the middle of its back: a huge, distinctly marked crown like the ermine ones you see on royalty. I gasped out loud, "*King-King*," and the tears poured forth. "My goodness, *King-King*, it's you," I said. I took my walkie-talkie, called Jack immediately, and told him what had happened. He said he would try to come home a little earlier and that I should take photos. It was about 6 am in August so the daylight was good. Part of me was afraid to leave

King-King in case he flew away, yet I knew I had to get a camera to document this event. I stood and looked closely because there were letters on the wingspan: A N N A.

I didn't know if A N N A had any meaning until Jack and I discussed it later. At the time of ***King's*** transition, I was having difficulty finding someone to help me clean the 3,000 square feet of building space everyday. I had found a lady who was extraordinarily good at cleaning, but Jack and I both felt that she was asking for too much money. The lady's name was <u>AN</u>na Lu<u>NA</u>, and I realized that ***King*** was telling us to hire her. So we did just that. (She has turned out to be one of my finest employees: loyal, dependable, and hardworking.)

I had taken quite a few pictures of ***King*** that special morning, talked to him, and cried with joy realizing that he had reincarnated and was showing himself to me with a special message – that he was still here and to hire A N N A. I stayed at the gate from 6 am to almost noon, but between 11 and noon the sun on the gate created intense heat. About 10 minutes before noon, ***King's*** wings were starting to collapse, and I was so afraid he was going to fall. I had conversation after conversation with him, and I felt ever so close to him. At 11:58 am, I was about to say my last goodbye, but I heard a flutter and ***King*** was gone from the gate, leaving a pollen residue behind. I then looked to the ground and saw him there. My first reaction was to pick him up and save him, but then I received the distinct message from God to let him be free. I leaned over ***King-King***, asked if I could touch him, and received the message that it would be okay. I gently touched him and got pollen on my fingers; within seconds,

66

this priceless butterfly flew up and allowed me to see that he was perfectly in one piece. He ascended into the oak trees, hesitated, and then fluttered out across the land. *King's* message had been delivered, and I knew he was still with me. Jack never got to witness this wonderful experience, but he developed the pictures when he got home and could hardly believe what he saw.

§

Jack continued to build houses for the cats who kept coming to our land and for those we adopted. Building on this land never ceased for 13 years (1994-2006). On this magnificent land inside the handmade gates that protect it, we honor every one of God's creatures. We allow peace to permeate all creation without human interference. (In fact, only a handful of people are allowed inside the gates.) We turn over June bugs to give them a fair chance at life. We provide for and nurture everything that lives here. I see myself as a Mother Theresa of the animal kingdom because I have taken down-and-out, transient, homeless creatures and passionately provided and cared for them. Both Jack and I willingly sacrificed our own needs to meet those of the animals, and they are our inspiration. All creatures here live in peace on sacred, protected, and cherished land.

§

CHAPTER 3

CONVERSATIONS WITH JACK:

THE CONTINUATION OF LOVE FROM THE OTHER SIDE

ILLUMINATION

I do not pray for the results
for only God knows
What they may be.
But I pray for the energy
to sustain my effort
toward the results
by the way of right action.

I do not pray to be spared failure
for who can know
what opportunity
an adversity may mask?
But I pray for the courage
to overcome failure
Again and again if necessary.

I do not pray for specific success
or achievement
But only for those signposts
that I am indeed following my path
and that my life is of use to others.

I do not pray as a means of asking for
But of giving thanks,
for prayer is the effect of thought
which occupies time and space,
and having seen
what therefore must be
Should I be less than thankful?

—Unknown

Jack and I began 2007 on a high note by writing our annual New Years Eve affirmations. We included our hopes and aspirations for the coming year and as always, tried to stay in favor with God. Jack's affirmations were professionally based and involved our construction company. Because Jack was responsible for earning our living, this particular affirmation was very important to both of us. My affirmations leaned toward **CAT HAVEN** and the needs of all the animals living there. Both of us wrote intentions to improve and grow personally within our relationship and on our own. We had a simple but happy "at home" New Years Eve.

On January 1, Jack and his truck were packed and ready for a journey to South Padre Island for two months of work. Our very best customers, Eric and Kelly, had hired him to work at their magnificent beach vacation home. This was the third year we had started the New Year with a good job, and we were very thankful. Jack was happy because the location of work afforded him the opportunity to kayak and participate in his favorite water sports on his off time. I was happy because I could take this opportunity to deep clean our house. It was a wonderful time of year for us. The land did not require much care, but the house did. The first year Jack and I were separated for this work was difficult for both of us; we both cried our hearts out when we parted. We kept in touch through walkie-talkies during his seven-hour trip, and I felt as though I was traveling with Jack the entire way. In the second year of this work, Jack left and only I cried. The third year he left for work, neither one of us cried.

(After Jack's return from South Padre, he

said to me one day, "I think you like living alone."
My response was, "No, I just like the perks – no
cooking, watching TV when I can't sleep. But no,
otherwise I do not like it!")

The first weekend Jack was home from his
work trip, we unpacked the truck and simply got
organized. The second weekend we did not go out
dancing because the weather was bad, so we started
planning for the future. Jack had a new project in
mind: to begin to flip foreclosed houses, something
for which he certainly had the talent. In fact, Jack
had been checking with banks to see what line of
credit we could establish. Although I was nervous
and had reservations about risking the routine of
our financial life, Jack made me feel comfortable
about the new projects. In fact, the very afternoon
he died, he reassured me and calmed my anxieties.
But then there was the dream.

*The morning of March 30, 2007, I awoke from
the worst dream ever. I was on a strange, old
ship. The waves were rough; I could feel the ship
sinking, the engine grinding. I looked outside and
saw many smaller boats tossing on the waves. The
front of my ship was only a few feet from being
completely under water; the back two thirds of
the ship were already immersed in the sea. I was
very afraid and could not find Jack. I saw plates
and dishes floating on the water and knew the
boat was sinking. Suddenly, I felt someone from
behind give me a boost up, and then I awoke in
tears.*

I moved over to Jack in bed and cried, "I
couldn't find you." He said reassuringly, "I'm here,

honey. I'm here." The warmth of his arms around me gave comfort, but I was still rattled by the dream. (I was told later that it was God who lifted me and that the other ships were obstacles I would have to overcome.) When I recovered somewhat, I realized that this was the second night in a row of a dream in which I couldn't find Jack.

Jack was extraordinarily industrious that morning. He cut down several large cedar trees and was happy to open new growth and natural bushes to the sunlight. Because of this, the bushes and trees would grow stronger and thicker, giving us more privacy to protect our babies and ourselves. We both laid the heavy cedar branches along the pathways I was creating with cypress mulch. The work looked great, and we were both pleased. Jack did a number of catch-up tasks, including putting into the ground a sign acknowledging *King's* favorite bush. Jack then told me he had a surprise, which was a heavy-duty rain gauge that was visible from the house. As the day progressed, Jack continued to finish all the chores we hadn't gotten to over the summer. It was as though he felt compelled to complete unfinished business. I remember Jack's loving hand on my leg as we snuggled together that afternoon on the couch, and he told me, "I would never do anything you're not comfortable with."

On the evening of March 30 because it was raining, Jack suggested that we go dancing for a short while, so we went down the street to a local café to listen and dance to one of our favorite rock-and-roll musicians. We made the short trip there, met friends, and ate. Jack jokingly asked if he could have some French fries, which weren't a part of our diet. Because they were homemade and this was a special night, I of course said yes. Jack told me that I would have some too, and I did. We were very happy to go out dancing because we hadn't done so since before Christmas. The first song was too fast for us that night (since we had just eaten), so we sat it out; the second song was an East Coast Swing (a favorite dance), so Jack led me to the dance floor. When we were halfway through the song, Jack appeared to trip. I was about to chastise him for the wrong foot pattern move, but then he hit the floor and I thought he had been knocked unconscious. Jack's head was bleeding and he was very pale. I leaned over and kissed him and told him not to leave me.

The next two hours were a blur. EMS workers arrived quickly and surrounded Jack; the police came; and someone told me to step away because the EMS workers needed room to tend to Jack. I was in total disbelief. People came up to me in support, telling me to breathe and trying to calm me. Because of Jack's size – the physique of a construction worker, very large but certainly not fat – it took several men to put him in the ambulance. I was told that I could not ride to the hospital with him, so I went in the police car. I had the presence of mind to call my best friend Phyliss Mangold, our neighbors Jim and Jean Sellstrom, and Eric and Kelly around 10:45 pm; they were kind enough to meet me at the hospital. We were all together in an emergency waiting room when at 11:40 pm, a female doctor walked in and pronounced Jack dead. I thought I was in a nightmare like the one with the ship and hoped I would soon wake up, but this was so terribly real.

I was allowed to see Jack for the last

time. My recollection is that Phyliss, Eric, and a young worker from the café went with me. Oh my God, I was paralyzed with fright. I kissed Jack's magnificent head and could see the wound (which I found out later was not the cause of his demise). Jack's hands – his incredibly soft and beautiful hands that did so much to make my life perfect – were still warm and pliable. I tried to remove his wedding ring, but it was a snug fit so someone else (I don't remember who) had to do it for me. Jack's wallet and keys were given to me, I believe. It's hard to remember exactly, as I was overcome with emotion. Unless you have gone through an overwhelmingly traumatic experience like this one, you simply can't imagine the sadness, shock, despair, pain, and grief.

It's difficult to describe the agony of leaving the love of your life's body lying on a hospital gurney, but I had no choice. At the hospital and outside the café when I returned to pick up Jack's truck, the café owner Curtis and other workers were very supportive of and sympathetic to me. It meant a lot; one of the employees, Chris, even drove me home.

A little after midnight alone in the house, I was literally going in circles. The first person I called was Audrey because I knew she would know how to handle me. We talked for quite awhile, and then I went in circles again. The phone rang around 2 am, and it was a beautiful lady's voice representing the Lone Star Lions Eye Bank. She asked if Jack would be a willing eye donor, and I said, "Absolutely, yes."

Jack's body then underwent over 48 hours of autopsy and removal of healthy corneas, skin, bone, and organs for donations to those in need. Just a year before his death, Jack had undergone scans at a heart hospital, which revealed no signs of an existing problem. However, the medical examiner who performed the autopsy later told me that Jack's healthy living and diet had extended his life but that his hidden genetic heart condition was going to be his downfall no matter what.

§

Around 9:00 the morning after Jack's passing, my brain and body were Jell-O while I waited outside the front gate for Phyliss to pick me up and take me to the bank. I looked up as a very large multi-colored butterfly came down from a cedar tree outside my property, flew at arms length in front of my face, and slowly went over the gate and up into an oak tree. While the butterfly lingered in the tree, I knew immediately that Jack was letting me know that his spirit was here on the land. What a thrill: my sweetheart was still with me!

Later in the day, dazed and debilitated from the pain of shock, I spoke with Phyliss for about the tenth time. She suggested that I write my thoughts in a letter to help ease the suffering. I rambled for pages, which began…

To Jack –
To my sweetest, dearest, most unselfish, thoughtful, considerate, and loving husband. Oh, how I miss you; perhaps you know. Perhaps you see me struggling to deal with the pain of the loss of you. Thank you, darling man, for working so hard to give me so much pleasure. Don't leave heaven until I get there – unless you come back as a hummingbird or new kitty…

After the initial shock of Jack's transition, I began to realize the many gifts he had given me. His greatest gift was acceptance. He never judged me – how I looked, what I did, or the way I did it. Jack never restricted me in any way, fully allowing me to be me. He never complained about my behavior, actions, or choices. He told me everyday, "I love you just the way you are." All this had been foreign to me before Jack came into my life. In my mind he was the most unselfish human being on the face of this earth, literally gave everything he made or had to me, trusted me completely, and SHOWCASED ME in all ways and in all places. I felt truly blessed to have had the best. Only now that Jack is in a new dimension do I see clearly his significance in my life and his LOVE – GOD'S LOVE – about which I knew very little until Jack came to show me.

On April 3 I drove my car for the first time since Jack's passing. My body was still weak and I was very hesitant to drive. As I backed out from the gate, I felt Jack take the wheel of the car. I knew it was he because of the way the car was steering itself. My hands were on the wheel, but I was not in control. This was the second time Jack revealed his presence to me after his transition.

§

During one of my many moments of despondency, fear, and pain in the grieving process, I cried out: "Oh God, what am I going to do? I have over 100 animals to care for and no income!" God's answer was, *"USE YOUR CREATIVE TALENTS, MY CHILD, AND I WILL GIVE*

YOU EVERYTHING YOU NEED." Well, I didn't know if I had any creative talents at that time. In fact, it was several months later when I told Shakti Miller – my healer and teacher – about what was transpiring, and she suggested I write a book.

§

I had pondered the importance of Jack's Easter weekend transition and decided to ask Audrey who in turn asked Kay Stahli, a fellow intuitive, about it. Kay said:

> *"HE IS RISEN.*
> *He made the ascension directly to heaven --*
> *no stops.*
> *He will not have to come back to this earth*
> *plane again.*
> *When you leave, you won't come back either*
> *and will be with him forever.*
> *He was doing his two favorite things:*
> *holding you in his arms and dancing."*

As soon as Audrey gave me Kay's quote, I told Jack out loud: "You're lucky you ascended into heaven. No stops on the way. You must have been surprised when you looked down and saw your body and all the people rushing around you. You will not be coming back to earth; what a blessing. And when my time comes to join you and be in your arms again, I WILL NEVER LEAVE YOU. We will be together forever." So Jack had mastered his lessons and was free to go straight to heaven without suffering through purgatory. My man was a pure spirit.

It was 10 days later when the results of the autopsy came back, which revealed the undetectable genetic defect that took Jack in the blink of an eye.

Before Jack was cremated (his wish), he looked his best in his new Capezio Brazilian dance shoes, favorite suede jacket, and silk shirt. On top of his body was a red silk dress and red velvet hat he had bought for me, plus my best dance shoes. (I had never paid $100 for a dress, but Jack wanted me to have this particular one because he said my butt looked great in it!) Jack went dancing into heaven. I keep his ashes in a beautiful hand carved wooden box, which he had purchased for me in Honduras the year before. I remember protesting that the box was too expensive but because Jack wanted to please me, he purchased it. Neither of us had any idea of its future purpose.

I also remember that immediately after moving in together in 1989, Jack had asked me for a box in which to put some personal papers. I didn't know what the papers were, and I didn't ask. But six months before his passing, Jack gave me the documents and said, "Put them in a safe place because they contain my VA records and you might need them." It turns out that the documents defined his secret mission in Vietnam, and they ultimately benefited me by providing a widow's pension.

§

Jack's generosity to the universe did not end after his transition. As a result of his cornea donation, two people can now see through those eyes of love. Also, Jack's healthy skin and tissue will be preserved for up to two years and can help as many as 60 to 70 people. The following is inscribed on a plaque I received from the Lone Star Lions Eye Bank:

My memories in the months following Jack's transition are still vivid. On April 4 (five days after Jack's passing), *Butch* – one of our orange cats – died. That day, as I was filling water jugs by a water hole he had used, I saw a vibrant yellow/ gold butterfly. I knew instantly that it was *Butch*. On the morning of April 6, I was sitting on one of the benches in *The Park*, very tired from yard work and filling wildlife water pans. I indicated for Jack – if he was there – to come and sit beside me on the bench. I bowed my head from fatigue and through flowing tears, looked up to see two butterflies coming toward me from an oak tree. One was large, white, and multicolored; following it was the same yellow/gold butterfly from two days before. I knew Jack and *Butch* were together, and this lifted my spirit.

The evening of April 6, exactly one week after Jack's transition, I made a life choice – not to be sad. I called Curtis at the café and told him this. Apparently, the band that night honored Jack with special music we both loved, and many in the crowd remembered him fondly. Also of special significance that night was the fact that *Ivy*, Jack's Siamese cat, allowed me to gently touch her. She had never allowed me to pet her before!

On April 7, I was worn out from working so hard. That evening I felt someone trip me, and I knew it was Jack. I then heard his voice say, *"You will not work tomorrow."* At this point I couldn't do much anyway because my ankle was hurt. So I rested for 24 hours and was ready to go again.

On April 12, I woke up laughing my head off after a radiant, joyful, loving dream. It seems the Disney people wanted to talk to and hire me for my ideas. Someone had given a glowing report of my talents. (I think it was an old boss.) Even though I knew nothing about computers, the Disney people were willing to accept my stories and experiences; they promised me a lot of money although I didn't hear the amount. There was a group of distinguished advisors sitting around taking notes on what I said. I woke up feeling wonderful. I knew I was going to be all right.

On April 16, I was blowing leaves in front of the house, where I saw a uniquely marked butterfly. For a few seconds, I watched it and smiled. The butterfly was slightly different in design and color than what I had seen before, but I knew it was Jack. (He was just wearing a different outfit). I turned the blower off, placed it on the driveway, and walked away 20 or more feet. When my back was turned, the blower started up on its own. I thought perhaps it had fallen and thus restarted, but I went over and recognized that this couldn't possibly have happened. I turned it off again and walked away. Then the blower came on a second time! It made me laugh and I asked Jack, "Are you playing games with me?"

§

During the first five months after Jack's transition, I made many painful observations about people. Here I was in the depths of despair, and I found myself having to deal with the surprising behavior of those I had thought were trustworthy friends and good neighbors. A few people stayed around for a couple of months until I realized they wanted to get something – such as Jack's vehicle, tools, and clothes – and then they were gone from my life. There were also those I had known and loved for years who didn't call. Perhaps the neighbors and former friends understood the storm and range of emotions that accompany grief. (My house cats could tell you a thing or two if they could talk!) I don't know, but it was a shocking awakening amid the pain of loss. Fortunately, because of Jack's donations of eyes, bone, and tissue after his transition, I was added to a mailing list to receive a magnificent series of information outlining the most helpful and accurate explanations of what to expect and when during the grieving process. These booklets, written by Doug Manning, were both timely and comforting. Doug Manning – who was kind enough to speak with me over the phone (not to mention the fact that I was lucky to get in touch with him) after I received the first booklet – helped me realize that my emotional outpourings were perfectly natural, and I am forever thankful for his help.

Also in these months as I was reeling from the shock of death, I struggled to deal with large corporation ineptness. To make a long story short, I tried to get one of the biggest and supposedly best telephone companies to disconnect our business phone lines, and it was a debilitating experience. Not only did this company take weeks to honor Jack's death certificates as proof of commercial closure, but when it finally did cut off the business lines, it mistakenly disconnected my personal phone as well. Furthermore, I continued to receive phone bills for five months after the business lines were cut off! I had similar horrible run-ins with gasoline credit card companies and subsequently got rid of several credit cards. It just goes to show that the larger the corporation, the worse the customer service.

Finding responsible and dependable young people to help with the wildlife refuge was an eye-opener as well. One by one, a few respectable, hardworking young men presented themselves, but many times I was stuck doing hours of physical labor alone (at age 72!) because workers didn't show up (or call to say they couldn't show up despite having cell phones) as promised. Many of the young people I dealt with were not reliable individuals – a sign of the times. Respect for elders seems to be more and more a thing of the past. I also see clearly that the world is not better than it was in my youth despite the abundance of technological improvements and supposed ease of living. The days of courtesy and consideration are dwindling, and I miss that.

§

On May 2 as I was sitting on the front porch,

the same large, uniquely marked butterfly from April landed on the white wrought iron table beside me. I talked to it as though it were Jack, and it moved to several different locations on the table. The next day, I was feeding *Ching* – a special, feral, Siamese cat – on what Jack and I called the "white deck." I saw this same butterfly on a small tree by the side of the deck and close to one of the buildings in **The Village**. Of course, I now KNEW it was Jack, so I extended my right hand while waiting for *Ching* to eat. The sun was shining in my eyes; I closed them and extended my hand. I told Jack, "If you are here, come sit on my hand." I was startled by a tickle on the hairs of my middle finger. I opened my eyes, and there was the butterfly on my hand! I gasped. It lingered for several seconds and then flew back to the same tree. I wept joyfully and laid my head against one of the 50-gallon food barrels. I again closed my eyes briefly. When I opened them, the magnificent butterfly was on that barrel close to my right cheek. *Ching* seemed startled; I believe she saw her "Daddy's" spirit. I was overwhelmed. I KNEW – I just KNEW – that my love was with us. The butterfly spirit flew back to the same tree and then soared straight up above my head into the oak trees. Oh my, how exhilarating to feel the presence of my beloved and of God! (Jack also sometimes appeared to me as a butterfly and greeted me against the lights of the gate when I arrived home at night, just as he did when alive.)

June 7, 2007 was the 19th anniversary of the day Jack and I had first talked on the phone. It was also the day I went to probate court. I was in my closet deciding what to wear that wasn't black when I heard a voice say, *"Wear something happy."*

On June 9, 2007 – the anniversary of our first date – I felt Jack's presence again. It seemed whenever I had workmen here (as I did on this day), Jack would show up in the form of a butterfly. In fact, workers would frequently point out his presence to me. Jack's appearance and color as a butterfly changed sometimes, but I still knew it was my love.

In mid-June I received a call from Audrey, who said that Jack was going to have a message for June 21, my birthday. He wanted her to write the message in a birthday card rather than tell me by phone. On the morning of June 18, Audrey called to say that Jack had both given her the message and made a selection from the birthday cards she had placed on her table. She mailed the card that day with specific instructions for me from Jack not to open it until the 21st. I excitedly opened my mailbox on June 20, and there was the card. I hurried home to the bedroom and placed it on Jack's bed pillow. It was all I could do not to open the card right then! I awoke at 4 am the next morning, turned on the light, picked up the card, and opened it. I gasped as I read Jack's words.

Hi Sweetheart -- Well this is certainly different from last year!! Roses, dining, and dancing. We had it all and I want to thank you for being what you are: intelligent, beautiful, spiritual -- making our home a haven. To enter at night was like walking into the peace among the storm. Now, my lady, you are doing the norm. It's okay to yell, scream, cry, laugh, remember, but it's time to be able to accept what is and move on. I am most pleased, sweetheart, to see you reaching out to others. As they cared and respected me, so they will be there for you. I love, love, love you and send you my strength, courage, and hope. Have faith in yourself, dear heart — I do.

Jack, Lady, and all that came before.
A HAPPY BIRTHDAY

Heavenly music

(*Lady* was our cat who had just recently died.)

I cried and I laughed and I cried and I laughed. I could see immediately why Jack selected the card that he did. It had smiling animals holding balloons all over the front. It was my best birthday gift ever.

On July 3, a butterfly was on the white chair outside the front of the house as I went to check on *Minnie* (a silver-gray cat, probably the oldest one on the land) after a heavy downpour of rain. The butterfly lingered, opened and closed its wings three to four times, and then happily flew over to the well. I needed that sighting because I hadn't seen Jack in awhile. The same butterfly – along with a black one I believed to be *King* – hung around all week, and it was wonderful.

A few months later on August 8, I was very down, tired, and hot. My hired helpers had left me in the lurch by not showing up for days when they said they would. I literally threw myself on the driveway and said, "God, please help me!" Immediately, a response came back: *"TRUST ME. ALL IS IN DIVINE ORDER."*

On August 17, I had a most unique dream – that a beautiful, gentle, dark-haired woman kissed me on the lips. It was not a sensual or sexual experience but rather a deeply comforting one.

Later, Audrey told me that an angel had kissed me.

August 19, 2007 was the first day I "listened" to Jack's answers to my talking and questions. I realized an entirely different union with him, sensing his presence and not feeling so alone. That same day, I was reading *A Course in Miracles*. I removed the book from my bed – where I had referred to it intermittently when I felt so low and needed direction – and took it to what we call the Crystal Room. I knew it was time for serious reading and review, and I felt an urgency to take action. I remembered how important the book had been to our relationship when Jack and I first met. We actually took 365 days and studied the course together. Even if Jack was working out of town, we discussed each day's reading that night. On August 19, MIRACLE #30 had my complete attention:

"By recognizing the spirit, miracles adjust the level of perception and show them in proper alignment. This places spirit at the center where it can communicate directly."

I said loudly, standing up and raising my arm: "I want to talk to my husband's spirit."

Message: You are.

Me: I choose to believe you are here, right now.

Jack: I am, sweetie, I am. I did not leave you.

Me: Do you know how much I love you?

Jack: I love you too.

Me: I miss you and your strength.

Jack: You are strong, and the right ones are coming to help you. Have no fear. I will see to it.

Me: Remember when we first read *A Course in Miracles*?

Jack: I sure do. It brought me close to you.

Me: It is bringing me closer to you now.

Jack: That's good. I am never far away. I would never leave you.

Me: Thank you. I need that.

Jack: Know that. I am your one true love. I will wait for you. I will never leave your side. Trust, sweetie, trust.

Me: We have an unspeakable love.

Jack: We do indeed. Wherever you are, I am.

Me: I want to see you.

Jack: You will when God tells me.

Me: Okay, I accept that and may God bless both of us.

Jack: Oh sweetie, have no fear that you are blessed. I see all you do. God sees all you do. Stop the sadness; it is not necessary. You will have time to do all you want to do, and I will be waiting for you.

Me: I want to be with you.

Jack: You are not ready. Our babies need you. Do the work and be happy doing it. Now, go to work. I am working too. KNOWING is more important than SEEING.

LATER THAT DAY

Me: I felt your presence and protection. For the first time, your lady took time to listen for you and to you. How about that! I have assured KNOWING you are here protecting me. My love for you is enhanced. The connection is there, forever. I no longer feel such deep pain of separation. Thank you for listening and responding to your wife. What a difference it made in my life today, what a positive difference.

AUGUST 20

(I was feeding deer on the white deck.)

Me: I know you are here.

Jack: *I am. I see you.*

Me: I feel you and it is wonderful. This is the best thing that has happened since you left.

Jack: *Remember, now, I never left.*

LATER THAT DAY

Me: It is so very interesting because my initial connection to you was never your body – though I certainly loved your towering stature standing beside me holding my hand, touching me anywhere, brushing the hair from my face, and dancing with me – but ALWAYS my connection was to your spirit and your heart. It was an instant – a holy instant connection – even through the phone and your magnificent gentle, peaceful, comforting, and yet familiar voice. I remember it so well. Yes, I know you are there, and my mind's eye sees you – every part of you – at once and all we did from Santa Fe, to London, the theatre, St. Paul's Cathedral, Windsor Castle, The Isle of Wight, the magnificent white albatrosses following the ship to Hawaii, Mexico, the shops, all the things you bought me, Jamaica, the Panama Canal, Costa Rica, and on and on. Seeing this land for the first time with you and remembering the card reader, Hoortie Adamson, who told me about this man I would meet whom I would instantly recognize through his eyes – your unbelievable, beautiful, deep, and loving brown eyes. I see them now. The first machete-cutting afternoon through the thick brush here on the land. Meditations on Easter Sunday and the triangular rock we found and placed where we thought the

89

house would be. The oak trees, majestic oak trees we uncovered through the brush. Oh my, what excitement. We had no money but we had each other and mostly your creative ideas and talent. With God on our side, we found a way to afford and build the house – I designed and you mostly constructed. What a life we made and what a journey we had. Time flies by when you are having a good time.

Jack: It's not over. We still have each other. You are never alone. I go with you everywhere. It's like South Padre Island -- you work there and I work here and we are together and will be for eternity. Remember that, for eternity with eternal forgiveness. In my eyes you can do no wrong. You are perfect and as I always said, I love you just the way you are. Just you and me babe, just you and me.

Me: You taught me to love.

Jack: Dorothy Ann Rose, I would never leave you -- never.

9:50 PM

Me: I am so happy to have you to talk to again.

Jack: I love to hear you.

Me: You are my joy.

Jack: You are mine too. I am happy to see you working happily today. Don't overdo it.

Me: I need help with *Ivy* tonight. Tell her to come in; she is not coming in at night the way she should.

AUGUST 21, 6:20 AM

Me: I am sitting on your potty.

Jack: I know. I like that.

Me: On the birthday card you selected for me,

you said you loved coming into the house at night because it was so peaceful, yet you had told me you did not like the perfection of my housekeeping. You still found peace in the house.

Jack: Oh yes. I knew that was the way you were and I allowed that. I wanted you to be the way you were.

Me: I feel guilt now.

Jack: Oh no, never feel guilt.

Me: I guess the fastidious cleaning was my attempt for at least some level of perfection – to do something right!

Jack: Oh, that makes me laugh because I know, saw, and lived with the perfection of you. Oh, sweet one, let those foolish thoughts fall by the wayside. You are oh so much more than those foolish fears.

Me: Oh, if I could do it all over again.

Jack: We would both do things the way we did because at that time, that is how we were. It is only by these experiences we learn and grow and change. Bless the experiences. I never loved you less because of what you did. I loved you because of what you were, are, and always will be: my one true love I had longed for, looked for, lived for since we were last together. Now we will never be apart. Always together, side-by-side -- I promise you. I watch over you as you sleep, as you work and go about your business. I watch those who come through the gate. I will protect you. Have no fears.

Me: I would like to sit here in the Crystal Room all day and talk to you. I see you come through the door and place your keys and change...

Jack: I am there right now.

Me: Massage my shoulders.

Jack: Allow me.

(I did, and I actually felt pain leave my shoulders.)
 Me: Thank you.

Jack: You are welcome. Stop slouching.

Me (with a smile): I will try.

Jack: Remember me telling you to stand up STRAIGHT?

Me: Okay, thank you again. I will have a better day now.

Jack: That's good. I want all your days to be good. You are a good woman, my woman. And remember I am always your man and (with a laugh) whenever you reach for me, I will do all that I can -- remember, we were headed for some place, somewhere we'd never been; but although we were frightened, we were ready for the power of love. It never ends, my darling; it only gets better. Remember my telling you that? For us, it has still only just begun. Have a joy-filled day. No more tears.

LATER THAT MORNING

(I touched Jack's shorts that were still hanging exactly as he had taken them off after kayaking, and I started to cry.)

Jack: No crying. I am not my body. I am free. I am as God created me. I am still here.

LATER

(I went to feed watermelon rind to the deer and was naked on the way to the outside shower.)

Jack: You look beautiful.

(I laughed out loud.)

Me: Do I need more readings?

Jack: No, sweetie, just listen to me. You always trusted me; trust me now. You have plenty to do. Do it and then we will talk. I tell you, the right ones are coming.

(Note: I have to laugh. Finally *Ivy* came in today, and she placed her weary body on the papers on which I was working. Maybe she saw Jack's spirit; she was so restless this morning.)

AUGUST 22

Me: Good morning, sweetheart. Are you there?

Jack: For you I am always here.

Me: I like to have this beautiful start to my day talking to you, feeling your presence.

Jack: Any time you connect to me is perfect.

Me: I am starting to have questions about your transition, sudden though it was. We were so happy having a good time eating and dancing.

Jack: I was as surprised as you were. I could not believe the flurry of people around me, and I did not understand why they were there.

Me: Did you have pain?

Jack: No, none at all. I was high. I was flying. I felt light, buoyant.

Me: Did you see the light?

Jack: Not right away. It seemed as though something or someone was not allowing me to get away.

Me: Do you suppose it was the emergency helpers?

Jack: It might have been.

Me: Did you see me and my fright?

Jack: Yes, and I felt you kiss me.

Me: I so wanted to do more to help you, but the EMS people would not let me. They wanted to do their work on you. Did you see Eric and Kelly, the Sellstroms, and Phyliss help me cope at the hospital?

Jack: I knew they were there, but my interest was only in you. I knew you kissed me and touched my hand. I knew someone gave you my ring. I was happy you had my ring.

Me: Are you aware your eyes were taken and now two other people have sight because of you? Two other people see through the eyes of love because of you.

Jack: Not really, but I am glad you told me.

Me: The doctor who performed the autopsy said the cells in your eyes were so perfect, and I was amazed because you wore glasses. Your eyes were pure and perfect.

Jack: Just like you my love, just like you.

Me: For two to three years your skin and bone grafts will help people. Isn't that amazing?

Jack: Yes it is, and I had no idea I would be so helpful to the universe.

Me: You were so courageous and I am so proud of you.

Jack: Your courage now far surpasses mine.

Me: Did you feel my presence at the funeral home when I placed white roses on your chest that Polly (a friend from the café) had given me? She said the roses were for two "perfect" people.

Jack: I did indeed, and I blessed Phyliss for standing beside you. She is a good and loyal friend. She loves you. I did not recognize how much. You can trust her.

Me: Did you feel pain in all of your physical donations to the universe?

Jack: Not a bit.

Me: You know you looked splendid as your body left the earth plane. You wore your favorite and best dances clothes, and my favorite and best dress, shoes and hat were lying over you. You literally went out dancing and – believe me – my spirit went dancing with you. You were not alone!

Jack: I felt it all. Your efforts were not in vain. My heart was light and I hated to see you so sad. Honey, your sadness is not necessary. I am happy and as Babaji said in a reading through Chris Carson, I have a newfound freedom so rejoice in it. Don't worry about me. I am here for you any time you want to tune in. I see it all, and I am so proud of you. Not one wrong thought have you had; and you continue to grow, grow, grow in understanding and patience. I am here, I am here -- I am here for you, at any time. I love to feel your presence toward me.

Me: This connection I believe will save my life because the disconnect broke my heart in many places, but I feel it coming together so that I can continue my work here and Our Mission. I will not let you down.

Jack: Oh how well I know that. You have my trust and many angels. You are an angel yourself. I was blessed to have found you again and spent so much time so close to you in the physical world. Now I am just as close in the spirit world. Nothing has really changed. We are close, we grow closer; it could not be better.

Me: I know you have work to do.

Jack: I do my love, I do. Have a happy day. Stay beautiful and care for yourself. I will always be with you.

Me: May God bless us.

Jack: Never fear. He is our help in every need.
Me: Not many people love me.
Jack: You don't need a lot of love from others.
Just love yourself; God loves you and know that
I love you.

AUGUST 23, EARLY MORNING
Me: Good morning, precious man. I know you are
here.
Jack: Yes, I am. I sense you are in haste today.
Me: I am. It is not that I don't want to spend tons of
time with you; Ann Pfeiffer is in town and coming
to see us this morning at 9:30. I have many things
to do before she gets here. My truck is full of cat
food because last night I just let the emptying of it
wait. I knew if I did it, I might regret it. I am trying
to learn not to do too much and to recognize my
human body itself for its limits.
Jack: I am glad to hear of that right thinking.
Me: Maybe we can come together later.
Jack: I will be here for you.
Me: I love you.
Jack: I love you too. Do enjoy our mutual friend
(Ann). She was one of the best customers, and I
know she appreciated my work. Go do what you
have to do.
Me: Tonight I want to talk about the new work you
are doing. Share with me what it is.
Jack: I will try to explain.

LATER THAT DAY
Me: I so long to be with you and your energy. I am
taking 30 minutes from working to sit down and
listen for you.
Jack: I am here. I always hear you. I know you do

not always hear me. It is necessary that you listen.
Many of us over here could be heard if our loved
ones would take the time to listen. I am so proud
of you that you made this choice. It is a lesson for
you; we both know that.

Me: Why can't you get *Ivy* to come in every
night?

Jack: She has her own needs to meet and besides,
I do believe she saw me the other morning and is
a bit confused.

Me: She did slip into the Crystal Room yesterday
on your box of kayaking clothes. I thought that was
interesting.

Jack: She is brighter than we give her credit for.

Me: I guess because I have the anticipation of Ann
coming, my thoughts are a bit scattered.

Jack: I understand, and I want you to enjoy
her. She is coming for some reason to teach you
something and perhaps learn something herself.
Have a beautiful day and know I will be there
showering my love on the meeting.

(Ann saw Jack's butterfly spirit at the gate when
she arrived. She thanked him so much for the
greeting.)

LATER
(August 23 is the date I arrived in this country in
1955 – 52 years ago today.)

Jack: I know I would have found you again
eventually but am glad I did not have to wait yet
another lifetime.

Me: I am just starting to understand the depth of
your love for me, to understand your wedding vow
promises and your wanting to be with me so much.
At the time I felt it to be somewhat possessive, even

controlling. Since I had been controlled so much of my life, I was slightly resentful. I didn't mean harm; it is just the way it was for me.

Jack: No need to apologize. I understand and as I have said before, I accepted you just the way you were. I was so happy to have found you again.

Me: I am glad I now understand so much better and will hold on to this feeling of wanting to be close to you forever more. I am your lady without hesitation.

Jack: I know, baby, I know. I see so many breakthroughs for you and it makes me happy. No regrets. You are learning so much so fast. I am happy and I am proud.

Me: I am sitting here on your side of the couch now. Your slippers are right where you left them. Everything is right where you left it. No one except the A/C man and alarm system guy has been in the house. Every footprint and fingerprint is yours and mine.

Jack: I enjoy hearing how you honor me. I see it, then you tell me, and it makes it doubly good.

Me: Ann Pfeiffer was here today, and I was so impressed with her thinking and the good conversation we had. I regret a little bit that she lives in Montana now because she and I would have spent a good deal of time together. I've always enjoyed talking to her. She is spiritually evolved and taught me that she is the caliber of friend I want to have.

Jack: You will (attract such friends), sweetheart, you will. Your vibration will bring them forth.

Me: She told me about a couple of dream discussion groups, and I might go.

Jack: You should. Don't hesitate.

Me: The Wednesday night one might be possible if it is not too late. I would not want to be out on dark nights.

Jack: That is a consideration, but let someone come pick you up.

Me: I will certainly check it out and let you know. Wait a minute; you will know at the same time I do. For your information and fun review, *Ivy* is in tonight, sitting in the Crystal Room on your kayaking clothes. She came in easily. *Hamlet* (our vibrant, orange/white house cat) is out, but he seems to be happy and able to take care of himself. This morning I found pictures of your magnificent arms holding *Hamlet* on the love seat, and it made me cry.

Jack: Don't cry, baby, please don't cry. It sets you back and you are doing so well. Keep going forward and upward.

AUGUST 24, 6:25 AM

Me: I overslept.

Jack: I am here, honey. I am watching you. Take your time. There is no hurry. I will be here.

Me: We have to give thought and energy to *Chloe* (a calico who lives in the *Ruffhouse*). She does not feel well.

Jack: I will do that. She will be okay.

AUGUST 25

Me: I only want to be with you. That is all I want – to be with you. I am so busy I don't have time to sit for even a minute. Maria (i.e., Anna Luna) is late and I am so stressed. I have a man coming over to evaluate the tools. I have to do the wildlife water and feed our babies. *Chloe* is at least walking today but not eating.

Jack: Don't worry, sweetheart. I am with you. I am here. I see it all. Feel some peace knowing that. I want you to calm down and realize I am with you at all times and in all places. I don't leave you. You leave me because you forget. My love is there and my energy is there; just remember and use it -- suck it up. You are not alone, baby, you are not alone.

Me: Thank you. As much as I plain love this place, the work level alone is overwhelming and my obsessive nature has me trying to do it all: water, animals, weed granite, clean and seal decks, blow all over, and on and on. I really need a couple of boys at least one day a week. Help me.

Jack: They are coming, I promise. They have made contact and are on their way. Don't despair; it hurts your energy flow.

Me: But now that I have found where I can reach you, that is all I want. A new friend through Ann Pfeiffer told me last night we have been together 14 lifetimes. Lucky 14. Remember, our wedding anniversaries are the 14th (of November).

Jack: I will never forget that; you can be sure.

Me: I don't want to do anything but talk with you, and the animals and work are getting in my way!

Jack: I have work to do also, and we will talk about that later. You are doing God's work, and right now it comes first.

Me: I think I just saw **King's** huge black and white butterfly at the back of the house near his bush.

Jack: You are right. He comes often to watch over you. Slow down. Baby, please slow down for me. We will not be on course for our next meeting unless you do.

Me: Okay, I will. It is just that there is so much I absolutely HAVE to do, and there is so much more I WANT to do with you.

Jack: God's work is the HAVE to right now. The Mission is the course. Divine order prevails, but you must slow down.

AUGUST 27

Me: Good morning, sweetheart. I know you are here.

Jack: I am always here; never doubt it.

Me: The right ones came this weekend. I almost passed out from the stress of trusting! The right computer guy to clean out your computer, what would appear to be the right tool guy who will take your tools on consignment...I have decided to sell all I can now while the tools have some value. Again, hopefully the right landscaping boy who will bring a friend next week was over Sunday, so I will have two boys. What a relief.

Jack: I could see your pain because of your perfection, and I am glad you have relief.

Me: You know all I want to do now is talk to you, but I have a destiny to fulfill and must be sure I go on meeting the right people so I can be on target to come to you when it is my time.

Jack: I so appreciate your dedication. You will not fail. I trust your judgments and your scheduling.

Me: Next time I want to talk about your work since you know about mine.

Jack: I will try to describe it. Continue with good days. You are making me so happy.

AUGUST 28

Me: Good morning, honey. Are you there?

Jack: As always, just waiting on you.

Me: We had a baby last night in my dream. Can you imagine?

Jack: We could have (had a baby together), but it was not meant to be. It may have caused us problems. We had waited so long to find each other; we needed to be a little selfish with our love for each other.

Me: I'm glad we were selfish. I don't think I could have shared you.

Jack: Me neither.

Me: The right ones came to empty your computer, check on your tools, and help with the yard. I was very disappointed last night when someone who said he wanted to buy tools didn't show up.

Jack: Let him go. He was not right. The plan is working well. Don't let the small stuff upset the flow. I am overjoyed at your progress. You are on target.

Me: *Chloe* is at the vet and is going to get X-rays today for her stomach. She has had no food for four to five days now and only weights eight pounds. I'm worried.

Jack: She is in the best hands, and the doctor seems to be trying to genuinely help you. Trust. Remember, whatever the outcome, it is God's plan and I am here to catch them all (the spirits of the animals). Today you are not hearing well because of your fears. Let go, sweetie. You do all you can always, and that is all God expects.

Me: I don't ever want to be without you.

Jack: Have no fear. Eternity it is.

AUGUST 29

Me: I want to tell you *Chloe* is better today, and I

want to know about your work.

Jack: It relates to engineering and testing of fabrics, materials.

Me: Yesterday I had a conversation with my father when I was working around the well.

Jack: Yes, he is here. I am with him at times. Be happy, love of my life.

SEPTEMBER 1

Me: I feel just a little guilt. I have not quite mastered this yet because my heart and soul want to be with you. Without your physical presence, there is so much to be done here; and although the right ones may have shown their faces, their time is restricted and therefore I have to do the work. I don't mind, yet it takes so much of my time.

Jack: I am here always, all the time. Whenever you need me, I am here for you. Do what you must, my love, and I have witnessed your incredible work this week. I see your deep love of the land and of me. I feel the depth and breadth of it. I am impressed by your love. Lady, my lady, you do no wrong.

Me: Where work is concerned, as much as I enjoy it, I don't know how long I am going to be able to keep it up.

Jack: Have no fear, sweetie, soon you will have companionship that will last and learn from you. Your every move and every wish will be replicated on the earth plane. There is another who will love the land as you do. I am watching.

Me: *Ivy* just came into the room and is looking around. She loves the green box where your kayaking shirts are stored.

Jack: Yes, she knows that I am here.

Me: My heart gets so heavy sometimes, and there are so many disappointments on the earth plane. No loyalty, just you and I. And without your physical presence, I feel a lot of pain. My heart gets heavy.

Jack: Remember, sweetie, it is the KNOWING that means everything, not the SEEING. Don't lose touch with that. Knowing is relief of all pain. My love surrounds you, as does God's. JOY JOY JOY.

Me: I have talked with Paul Minar (a friend and numerologist) two times this week; seems he is assured of coming to town sometime to make a presentation.

Jack: Yes, I know, and he will. You can trust him for sure. He is a gentleman.

Me: You know I don't want a lover; that's not my need. I just want a helpmate – someone to share all I do and feel, and also whom the land is deserving of. It could be a woman, for all I care. But I need physical support. Help me.

Jack: It is all a part of the plan. It is your patience that needs to be enhanced. God will never let you down. TRUST, TRUST, TRUST.

LATER THAT DAY

Jack: Sweetie, slow down.

Me: Sometimes I lose faith in my ability to talk to you this way. I cannot believe that I'm doing this. I cannot believe that I'm smart enough.

Jack: Oh, that is funny. You don't have to be smart; you just have to know God. I see your intentions to do so much and as I told you earlier, you need to slow down because this hampers our communication. Your heart gets heavy, and it should be light like it was when we started

104

communicating this way. I love to see you happy, and I see those who come into your space are full of light when you are. Keep shining; you are a beacon among the darkness. I see those who recognize this light and those who shy away. Your friends are changing because you are changing, and it is all good. Have no fears; all is well and unfolding as it should. Mr. Minar told you today you are mighty, and he is right. He is good for you. He will have great success. His intent is pure. You will be good for each other.

Me: I dreamed about your arms today – your left arm – and I felt it and kissed it.

Jack: I felt it too. I feel everything you kiss in my honor. I see everything. You are a walking angel. Those who reject you are in wonderment. You never offend.

(I began to feel like I took Jack for granted.)

Me: Sometimes I feel I don't have enough time to do all I have to do and the things I want to do like honoring you in written form.

Jack: Never worry about me. I am free and enjoy watching you grow. I know you are my woman, but live as you choose.

Me: You never controlled me ever when we were together in this lifetime, and I doubt if you did in the other 13 lifetimes we shared. I want to be more like you.

Jack: Just be like you; that is all God asks.

SEPTEMBER 4

Me: A bird flew into the glass door of the cat room at the house. *Ivy* saw it from inside. I ran outside and picked it up and held it in a green cloth as it took its last breath. I cried for all the birds in the world that I love. There is a lot of pain on the earth plane.

Jack: I caught his spirit; he felt no pain. Pain of death on the earth plane is imagined.

Me: I never seem to be able to relax.

Jack: You have plenty of time. Don't wear out your body before it's time.

SEPTEMBER 8

Me: I see you and feel you all the time, sweetheart.

Jack: I see you too. Don't be sad. We are still connected at the heart and that is all that matters.

Me: I have a wonderful book I want to finish reading for the second time about this man who spent 90 minutes in heaven and came back to earth to fulfill God's purpose – painful but powerful. I sometimes feel that's what's happening to me. This experience is painful but powerful. I just don't know if my experience is helping anybody else.

Jack: If you help one, that's all you need.

SEPTEMBER 12

Me: I was looking at photographs of us while I was cleaning today. I wished I had kissed you more.

Jack: It just made every one more special.

SEPTEMBER 13

(During the course of our conversations, I had asked Jack on several occasions, "Why don't you come to me in my dreams?" He always responded, *"When God allows it."*)

A dream…

I had traveled somewhere with a group of what appeared to be like-minded people. We were late, through no fault of our own. I went to the bathroom, I looked in the mirror, and everything about me seemed to be perfect. I was surprised at how little I needed to do to freshen up. I felt I looked good, which for me was not a usual sensation. I went outside to find the dining room. I saw a younger man waiting for me, and I felt I knew him. It was a hotel lobby meeting, which is where I met Jack. The young man was grand looking: tall, slim, and with beautiful eyes. He was smiling and assertive. He took my hand to shake it in a friendly way, and it felt softly familiar. He then escorted me to the elevator and stared at me just the way Jack would do. He looked professional, prosperous in many ways, and experienced on this earth plane. He was a temptation unrequested and unrequired by me, but there was also a perfection I was resisting. When I fully recognized the softness and touch of his hands, I knew it was Jack. God was allowing me to both see and touch Jack. The temptation was so great and so overwhelming. It was my one true love I started to cry.

Jack: Don't be sad, honey. We touched and it was magic. I feel a closeness like never before. The connection is even greater than before.

Me: At first I rejected your perfection in my mind – all I ever wanted – and then I recognized the touch of only your soft, soft hands.

Jack: And I yours. God said it was time. There will be many more (meetings) in our new work together. We have been blessed on earth and in heaven. Yours always.

Me: Through tears of joy I am not sad, I am in overwhelm – just like you said the first night we met. Now I understand our connection and the higher purpose. Like Audrey told me last night: I have a new career, and we have a new future together. Oh my.

Jack: Yes, it is a miracle to be working with you again. We always worked well together. Look what we accomplished on the earth plane together. Now let's see what we can do from this perspective. I am here whenever you need me.

Me: Now I can laugh at this new intensity of togetherness and love it.

Jack: Partners for eternity.

SEPTEMBER 15

Me: I want you to know you will always be my husband. My love for you grows and grows and grows deeper and wider beyond description and beyond belief. You are out of sight but most definitely not out of mind. Your value to my existence is seen more clearly now – perhaps the lessons of our many lifetimes together. I guarantee you will not have to look for me ever again. You know where I am, and I will come to you when the time is right. I promise.

SEPTEMBER 19

Me: I know you know we are starting to write a book honoring how we came together in this lifetime after waiting so long to find each other. I like to think I manifested you because of my wish list of the things I wanted in my man. At the beginning of our relationship before we were married, I remember introducing you at a party as "my man" and you seemed to be so pleased.

Jack: I was honored.
SEPTEMBER 28

I thanked God from the bottom of my heart for my wonderful life and apologized to Jack for being such a doofus and not understanding his needs and their depth. The fact that his soul still blends with mine is exhilarating, yet I have lingering guilt that I misinterpreted him.

Jack: I am laughing my head off. You are one of the most compassionate, caring, loving, giving women the earth plane has ever known. With all those gifts for me, what else could I have asked for? Have no regrets, sweetie. Our togetherness was and still is the perfect love. No one can ever compare to you. I watch you work without consideration of self -- that selfless loving for those creatures. You are my goddess. My love deepens as I now see you from God's level. Your journey home will be straight.

OCTOBER 6

Me: I want to talk to my husband's spirit.

Jack: You are, baby, you are.

Me: I feel a little bit empty like my tanks are all low.

Jack: Fill them with love for yourself. You have been neglecting yourself. That doesn't make me happy. Rest and spend time on yourself.

Me: I miss you so much. There are many things I do and when I'm busy, I forget a little bit. As soon as I rest, I think about the beautiful man and husband you were to me: absolutely perfect.

Jack: You were and still are perfect, but you are giving too much of yourself away.

Me: Sweetheart, I want to feel your presence. Calm my heart down; it is racing. (I took a breath and felt more peaceful. Jack's presence in the room always did that for me.) This week I found new homes for the bunnies. (Jack had found five California silk rabbits on a country road while releasing trapped raccoons away from our house.) We gave them two very good years, but the work was too much with the winter coming on – Maria and I standing in the rain to clean up their mess. It's surprising how little sadness I felt when they left. I believe a new space and place was going to be good for them too.

Jack: You always did a good job, but know it is time now to consider yourself.

Me: I also sold a few of your clothes. Your white dinner jacket was bought by Jim Covington (a contractor who worked for us); remember how considerate he was when we repaved our driveway last year. Apparently, he and his wife are cruise addicts too. His arms are long like yours, and everything you had fit him well. I realize it is just stuff with no value anymore to me. You enjoyed it but now someone else can. *Ivy* is not very much fun for me some days. I hope she's happy with her simple life. I almost have to fight to pet her.

Jack: Do your best, but do not interrupt her process.

OCTOBER 10

Me: Today I took myself to see Dr. Yong Cui at the Texas College of Traditional Chinese Medicine for an acupuncture session. I was feeling so out of balance. Probably six months of grieving and working at an unreasonable pace on the land, in the buildings, and with the animals was taking its toll on my body. The clinic where you and I went last year has been relocated to a brand new building, which is definitely beautiful – exquisite Chinese art, screens, and wall hangings all imported from China shiny and new. While lying on the table, I could feel your presence and the tears fell. I couldn't wipe the tears away because my hands were covered with needles. I heard you say, *"I am so glad you are taking time for yourself."* I knew you were happy that I was endeavoring to relax, and I received quite clearly the message you gave for Dr. Cui. The message was, *"I like the new clinic and the quality of service you offer. You deserve a beautiful space."* Now for your information, I delivered the message you had for the doctor. Dr. Cui bowed respectfully and turned to the right where I knew your spirit to be, and obviously he did too. He honored your presence with thanks. I found this to be so charming, and I was grateful in my heart.

§

That afternoon I decided I needed a treat for supper. I felt I wanted a selection of food because I hadn't been eating very well. I took myself to a local Chinese buffet and sat alone, which is what I wanted. It seemed that the busy hour had not begun. I noticed the music playing and found myself saying the words of the song, " I will stand by you, I will stand by you, I will never desert you, I won't let nobody hurt you." I said, "Oh my goodness!" I recognized the significance of the words Jack wanted me to hear and that he was speaking to me through music. Needless to say, there were tears over my supper, and I was glad the waiters had placed a double batch of napkins on the table because I sure needed them. Jack had been standing by me all day, and I felt it.

On October 11, I went for my annual

physical. My gynecologist asked politely, "How are you?" I looked behind me because I didn't know to whom she was talking. I said to myself, "How am I? I have no idea." I was not even on the list of being cared for. I burst into tears because I had no idea how I was. I could tell you exactly how all my 58 cats and their buildings were, how the projects on the land were, and which buildings had and had not been painted. But how I was and how I felt was not on my schedule. After a routine annual checkup, I was shocked to find that there was a small lump on my right breast. I did have a lingering problem in my right foot, which had become agitated in recent months. I had on my right hand a small ganglion, which too had become magnified within recent weeks. I was noting that my body weaknesses were all on the right side. Through some of my studies, I knew that the right side of the body represents the male energy. Well, I had just lost my beloved husband, so everything was manifesting on the same side of the body.

Because my brain is not medically oriented I choose alternative medicine to maintain good health. I therefore decided to get a breast thermography. The result was a fibroid cyst, which I believe came about because of Jack's departure, my perfectionism in cleaning and working the land, and trying too hard to keep things the same. I had been doing both Jack's work and my work alone, sometimes laboring physically for 10-12 hours a day for six months. (His energy empowered my body to perform at this level.) By caring for over 100 animals with food, water, and medicines, I had ignored my own care and attention.

Outlines in Louise Hay's book, *Heal Your Body*, explain the manifestation of a breast cyst and how to combat it through affirmation:

> **"I take in and give out nourishment in perfect balance. I am important. I count. I now care for and nourish myself with love and with joy. I allow others the freedom to be who they are. We are all safe and free."**

OCTOBER 12

Jack: Have no fear. Absolutely have no fear. It is a manifestation of lack of love for yourself. That is why I always tell you I am happy when you do things for yourself. You deserve. You need to slow down this pace and take care of you. You are all that matters to me. Your beautiful body needs attention; take time to observe and give it what it needs. There is time for everything you want to do, believe me. Let go and let God have his way. It is the best and the right way. Let go of the lists I always hated and do things as they come. Planning ahead is not what God wants. Live in the moment, this moment. Living in this moment is all there is. You can do that. That is all you have to do to dissolve this seeming problem. It is not a problem in your body, just in your mind. Let go. I will help you, baby. I don't like to see this level of distress. Stop now, I beg of you. It is not necessary.

Me: Should I do this mammogram?

Jack: If it shows what is already clear that there is nothing to fear, go ahead. You don't need the opinion of so many people, but I know how you are.

Me: If you were by my side telling me I was okay, I would be fine. But then if you were here, I would not have this problem.

Jack: I am there and you don't have the problem -- only in your mind. Trust me, trust me, trust me.

Me: I am going to talk to Datha Farrington in a few minutes.

Jack: That's good. She knows what to say. I love you. Please, sweetheart, don't worry anymore. As I always seem to say, it is not necessary.

On October 13, I made the following affirmation – I am grateful for how God is allowing me to be me, and I am going to be the person God wants me to be. I will overcome every adversity; I will fulfill my destiny; then I will go and be with Jack.

October 14 was a day for deep emotional cleansing – mother criticism pain and first spouse judgment pain, both of which were still held in my body. I wanted to release every bit of it. I also thought about the great gift God gave me when he led me to Jack. In my life there had been over 50 years of no acceptance, and then Jack taught me how to love myself. I knew that now more than ever, I needed to remember his teachings.

Me: Honey, are you there?

Jack: Yes, baby, I am. You seem to have to work so hard when the job is so easy. You have so much beauty inside and out. It was my pleasure loving you. I still do and will forever. I do see the benefits of releasing old hurts you still carry. Many have left today. You will lose them all. This is what you do so well when you focus on you. I am by your side in all healing. Never forget that. Just TRUST.

Later that day, I was thinking to myself, "I'm 72 years old, and only now am I understanding all the foolish mistakes I've made in my thinking all these years." I had finally let go of my mother's programming and the continuation of control from my first husband. I forgave myself for allowing this and I forgave my mother, who told me this very day how much she loved me. I forgave my first husband and my son, who is upset and doesn't understand why I left his father. I asked God for forgiveness – on my knees and on the hard ground – this day, and I believe he granted it. What a silly woman I had been to think I was less then perfect. A child of God is perfect, but I allowed the influence of others to affect my thinking. No more. All things were now working together for my good, and I thanked God for this opportunity to grow.

LATER

Me: Jack, are you there? I don't feel you.

Jack: You need to get yourself out of the way. The power that is in you is stronger than the power that is in the world. You are a powerful woman and need to clean up a few more things before you will be getting on with your life. You must heal yourself before you can heal others. We cannot do our work until your body is ready. You have become worn down and need to rebuild. You will do it well, as you always do. Think of the pain you now understand that you didn't before. Think of the understanding you have of others that you have recently experienced. Your work has only just begun. I am with you; I will be with you always and forever. Right now you must take time for you. You have such value to the world; you have

115

no idea. I feel I opened your heart to the beauty of you. Now you have to nurture yourself as I would. You resisted me; we both know that. Resist no more, my love. No more fences, no more walls. Resist no more. Surrender to the will of God. All is well and in divine order.

Me: Your room and your chair are my new space of comfort. Our photos surround me – what happy memories that I cherish so much, all wonderful memories. The picture of us and the never ending open tunnel of doors…I see myself coming to you through those doors to do more work together and then join hands forever. Strength comes to me when I think of working with you. So I must get well. The world needs our healing power. I am your lady and you are my man, and don't ever forget it!

Jack: I am smiling and thinking of our wedding days. The joy I felt seeing you come to me. Never forget, sweetheart: the power of love, our love, God's love for us. He is mighty pleased with you, and so am I. Don't cry, baby. If you could do one thing for me, don't cry any more tears.

Me: I went to Dr. Douglas Stakes today for the neck and fainting spell I had last night. I thought I was going to die. I was frightened. I wanted to be with you but could not bear to think of leaving our babies yet. They need special care like me, and I joyfully extend it to them and now to me.

Jack: Sweetie, you will outlive them all. You will have the perfect Stewards lined up and all those darned directives written; take my word on it. God knows what you want and he wants that too. It is all pure goodness and perfection of Our Mission. You can and will do it. I am telling you: you are preparing yourself for a monumental task with me by your side. Your wisdom, passion to heal, and compassion -- your greatest personal gift -- will be used by God. Know my love surrounds you. Feel it and get strong again.

Me: When I talk to you, I am whole and well.

Jack: Then talk any time you want. It is just you and me, babe; remember.

Me: I could not have had a better partner. You are the best.

OCTOBER 23

Me: I just made an appointment to see Dr. Douglas Stakes and his wife Janet on Halloween to review the results of the thermography digital screening.

Jack: Don't get dramatic. Just do what you have to do and know all is well.

Later that day, I repeated an affirmation to myself while walking down the driveway. I said, "God, I definitely accept my part in your plan for my salvation. You can trust me on that." God responded, *"THEN WHY DON'T YOU TRUST ME?"* I was knocked back.

That night at 8:00, Jack and I sent healing energy to a friend of Audrey's in North Carolina. I took Jack's right hand in mine and moved it to my heart. It didn't take long before I felt and saw bubbles of light with pearly colors bursting from my heart. They simply popped toward Audrey's friend. I called Audrey and told her that I felt silly that I had seen these bubbles. The following day Audrey's friend called and said that as she was packing her suitcase, she saw bubbles of light come to her. Of course, Audrey then told her that Jack and I had sent this healing energy the night before.

OCTOBER 26

(I was at the point of wanting to hear God's words.)

Me: Honey, I think I'm getting it. I'm beginning to feel the confidence that God is not going to take me away from Our Mission until it is complete. He just wanted me to slow down and honor me because I am important to the universe. I know I have the inner innate power to heal with you by my side. You are there and I am here. I feel myself changing, getting better. I feel a burden being lifted from my spirit. KNOWING *is* better then SEEING. Incidentally, I saw you flutter, Mr. Butterfly, when the tree trimmers were getting ready to leave. I know you approve of the work I am having done.

Jack: Yes I do, sweetheart. A good investment; everything looks very good, and the work level for you and Maria will be less. I support anything that supports you.

Me: I love this land, Jack, and I look forward to meeting the right Stewards who will love it the way we do. According to a report card from God, which Audrey has just done, **CAT HAVEN** will be here forever. We can watch over it together when I join you.

OCTOBER 29

Me: Last night I felt your presence here, I saw you here with me, I thought I touched your body, I felt I kissed you, I felt we talked, but I felt you didn't really want to stay. You didn't seem to want to dance. Am I right on all of this?

Jack: Yes, my darling lady, you are right. God allowed this because you have worked so hard to find the right answers and were a little low in spirit. I was with you so you were able to see and feel all that you did. And you were right: as much as I love you, here I am working with God and there is nothing like it. You will know one day when you join me. I am dancing. I feel tears for you; don't feel them for me. You have my promise that I will never leave your side and I am here for you at all times, but understand and accept that I am here and I am happy here. All I want is you to be happy there until we meet again. I will catch your spirit when you enter heaven. I will be first in line. Rest assured, mine will be the first arms to surround you.

Me: Wow. I know how much you love me, but it is bringing my heart peace to know that you are in a happier place. I want so much for you to be happy and understand your wish is the same for me. I know when you were with me in the physical how you rejoiced at little things I did for myself. Sometimes I felt selfish, but it made me happy. You never denied me when you were here, so why would you deny me now? It's my stupidity when I feel guilt. Let there be no more guilt; right.

Jack: Hooray, you finally get it!

Me: I know that everything I do now is to please God and make you proud of me. I want to do God's work. I want to be the way God wants me to be. I am trying to take the adversities I am experiencing and turn them into blessings because I know that it is what God wants. He is molding me, and I accept this period of being in a valley rather than on the mountaintop. I know God is with me and you are too. (Laughing) It was just easier when you were present in the physical. You helped me so much with your presence, your words, your hands, and when you carried me and one time rented a wheelchair (when I had surgery years ago). It was oh so comforting. I don't ever want a wheelchair again and expect you'll see that I don't have to have one. But just to let you know: you did everything, and it means so much to me to feel your loving care. I never had that feeling before you. Golly, what a good husband you were. How richly blessed I was to have deserved you. Back in June on the birthday card message, you said it was time to accept what was and get on with my life. Well, it has taken me another four months to get to the point of acceptance of your suggestion. It doesn't change my love; in fact, my love for you is intense beyond words, but I will open myself to what God has ready for me to enjoy and know you will enjoy that too. Just be here to share it. I want you to be part of absolutely everything I do. I do not want to have any feelings or do anything that you do not know about: no walls and no fences, from you or God. I want to feel freedom from all ties that have bound me. I want to live in spirit as God intended. I want to be free as God intended me to be. I want my broken heart to mend and be stronger than it ever was. They say when bones break and heal they are stronger at the breaking point, and that is what I want for my heart. You will always be my one true romantic love, but I can open myself to love of other kinds while on this earth plane: helpful love of the animals, land, and whatever God shows me. You will see and you will know, no secrets. You have my heart forever. Hold it in your loving hands next to your heart. Mend it, protect it, nourish and care for it; it will always be yours. CALM it as you do so well. Don't let me be too dramatic and waste its energy. Only you know its secrets. My heart is yours.

Jack: I will treasure it and the secrets and be thankful that you finally surrendered it to me. It's what I always wanted. We are now truly one, and I thank God for the gift of my lady's heart. We can do our new work as one; no more searching for you in other lifetimes. I have the greatest gift you could give me: your heart. I am fulfilled.

Me: You and God have my heart, never never never to part. We three are one, for eternity and so it is. My man, I will see you in heaven. THE END, OR SO I THOUGHT…

§

CHAPTER 4

IT ONLY GETS
BETTER

ILLUMINATION

"There is no death, but there is a belief in death."
A Course in Miracles

"Death is nothing at all. I have only slipped away into the next room. I am I and You are You. Whatever we were to each other, that we still are..." Anonymous

"You see dying is progression to a higher level. The possessiveness of life, selfishness, jealously, resentment -- these have been dropped with the old garment of the body. . Spirit now has new work to do. So have we -- to make the most of the rest of our lives until we join you." Anonymous

The same morning of October 29 after my early conversation with Jack, I continued my mission work with the animals. About four hours later, I walked into the kitchen and witnessed something extraordinary. At the kitchen counter are two large, heavy, high-backed, oak barstools. Earlier that morning – for the first time ever, I believe – I had sat on the left barstool to eat my breakfast. That stool was Jack's, where he ate almost every meal and watched the news on television. It is almost impossible to knock over these stools. The weight, leg shape, and placement make them very sturdy, stable seats. Nonetheless, I found his stool lying on its side away from the other stool. Neither of my two house cats was inside; and even if they were, their weight could not have unbalanced the stools.

Me: What, so I can't sit on your stool?

Jack: You can sit on my stool any time, baby. No, I just wanted you to know I AM STILL HERE.

§

And so continues the process of slowly, daily putting the many shattered fragments of myself back together again. Jack is still here working with me on Our "New" Mission to make the world a better place. Our conversations continue and are simple, yet of profound comfort to me. Our love continues to grow; though out of sight, Jack is never out of my mind. Our joy goes on in this new work of channeling healing energy. It is the togetherness that means everything, and the purest purpose enhances my soul.

NOVEMBER 14, 6 AM

Me: Good morning, sweetheart. It's our wedding anniversary today. It's difficult to be happy without

125

you, very difficult. And as you know, my sadness, my fears, and a little bit of resentment at being left alone with all that I have to do has manifested in some body weaknesses. I can handle them all, but without you to support and care for me as you always did, the sadness and fear of not being able to do all I want and have to still lingers. It is so difficult to be radiantly happy. I am grateful indeed for all I have, but the joy is hidden. I'm telling my tale of woe assuming you are there.

Jack: Yes, baby, I am here and I am so sorry for you. You are mighty brave. God watches over you and your worst fears will not be. This is a slowdown and readjust-your-priorities time. Balance your time with the Mission and yourself seems to be your main lesson.

Me: Audrey said you had a message for me on our anniversary, and I am not really hearing it at all.

Jack: You try too hard at everything. Allow me to speak. Allow things to happen. Don't try so hard to make them happen.

Me: I am just sad. I do still have fears, but the resentment is gone. I know you are with God and happy, and *my* choice is to remain here with our babies. They are my choice right now. I could not leave **Ching** and **Minnie** and **Morgan** (our white angel) or any of them. So this is where I will be. Today – our special day – for me and for you I will celebrate by attempting to release sadness and fears and fully recognize lessons God is giving me to learn. I believe I am smart enough to know them all and can actually laugh. There are so many! I am grateful to be aware of these lessons and want to get out of the muck and mire. I know God does not want me to suffer and struggle so. I will do my best to let go. Maybe you are doing God's work right now because I sure don't feel you with me. You say you are always here, and perhaps I am so full of my stuff that I cannot feel you. It's my problem and not yours. I will come back when you call me and when I can hear.

NOVEMBER 14, 6:25 PM

Me: I honor my sadness and my love for you. Both are so real and so deep. Part of you for me is lost. I felt sad on the Isle of Wight; I believe you had left me in another life also. Sadness can knock you to your knees as it did to me on the island. Our love was one-of-a-kind and still is. Damn, damn, damn, I miss you. I'm not the same without you. I am good – very good – but not the same. It's this difference of me that I have to adjust to. You gave and added so much to me and my life. It's a new life now, and I have to adjust. Manifestations of weaknesses…I know I will survive them and with God's trust will heal them and surprise anyone who knows me. Just me and you. Today I put my trust, my belief 100 percent in God. You have stepped aside to be sure I do just that. Yes, I KNOW you are there; but you have cleared the way for me now to go directly to God, to talk to God and not just to you. That is what you must do in order that I might get my priorities straight. From now on, I talk to God and you will listen. The three of us will be partners, for I know you are by His side and mine. It will be interesting. You proved your love to me, for me; and you took care of me. I need all of that and am now opening myself to the love of God completely. I need support. I need direction. I trust God to be there for me as you were and still are. But God has to be my man now, and we both know it. Yes, we both know it. I KNOW you are still there, still with me. You are with God, and I want to be partners with him too. Introduce me to God as your special lady, and maybe with both of you on my side I can get some healing. I'm having to let go and let God step in and care for me. I don't have many troubles but if I can get help in healing my body, I will work on my mind and balance my act here on earth. I will always do my share. I never expect anything for nothing. Today I will dedicate to our partnership and expect healing. Thank you.

NOVEMBER 16, 7:50 PM
(I did something enjoyable; can't remember what.)
Me: Oh, that was fun.
Jack: That's good, baby, have fun. You and Audrey both need to let go and have more fun. You have gone as far as you need to go with studies. No more studies. Have more fun.

NOVEMBER 17
Me: This is what I need in the way of physical support: someone who loves the land, knows how to care for the land, and can do the necessary repairs. My joy and happiness is this land, but I need support caring for it. Remember how I used to wish for an American Indian because we believed this was an old Indian burial ground?
Jack: Everyone will come that you need. Just feel the light that you are. I love you. God loves you. Lean on me, baby. Trust me and trust God. Surrender, my sweet, surrender to the Will of God.
Me: Okay. This day – November 17, 2007 – I

surrender all my needs, hopes, and wishes to the Will of God. God is in charge and all is well. Thank you for miraculous healings of me. I want to do my new work with you (channeling healing energy from both sides of the veil) but must first heal my own body, and it is done. I trust.

NOVEMBER 19

"Souls on all levels engage in another important activity when they are alone. They are expected to spend time mentally concentrating on helping those on Earth (or other physical worlds) whom they have known and cared about. From what I can gather, they go to a space some call the place of protection. Here they enter an 'interdimensional field of floating, silvery-blue energy,' and project outward to geographical area of their choosing. I am told this is a mental exercise in 'holding and releasing positive vibrational energy to create a territory.' _This means souls ride on their thought waves to specific people, buildings, or a given area of land in an attempt to comfort or effect change._"
–from *Journey of Souls* by
Michael Newton, PH.D.

(I dreamt that Jack walked from the well house to the main house.)

Me: Honey, was it true, last night you came by in my dream?

Jack: Yes, it was. I wanted you to know I approve of everything you have done. The place looks remarkable, and I am so proud of you. Rest for awhile. You will be fine. I am happy you are asking for help. The young man who came on Sunday is also the right kind of help you need. He is honorable and will be there as often as he can. If others have fallen, leave them alone.

Me: My love for you just gets better.

Jack: I told you so. Just because you don't see me doesn't mean I don't know all of this and feel it too. My heart is wider and deeper, and I too see everything you do and think, just as God does. I did not see it all when I was on the earth plane, but now I do. I too was blessed to have found you yet again. Next time our togetherness will be for eternity.

Me: It seems our energy channeling session really helped Audrey two days ago.

Jack: I will join you whenever you ask.

Me: I want to be selective.

Jack: I understand that choice.

Me: Maybe some healing energy for me today; tonight we will work on it. Our babies are waiting for me now.

THAT EVENING

Me: Any time you can give special attention to healing for me and my body, I would greatly appreciate it. Dr. Valenza (podiatrist) took care of my feet today. I'm getting new orthotics. Later I believe I will have the painful bursa removed from my right foot because it is a handicap to my movement and walking ability.

Jack: I think that's a good idea for you. You can handle it alone. Trust me. But if you want someone to drive you, go ahead. Your hand may need a little more time to rest.

Me: Do you think I will have to have surgery on

my hand?

Jack: No, I don't. Don't fill yourself with fear, sweetie. It is not God's plan for you to suffer and struggle. God wants you to turn aside from the fear of others and trust in Him completely. No matter how it looks, trust God and your inner beliefs.

NOVEMBER 20, MORNING

When you're lost in the abyss of grief, you sometimes forget what you know well including your own name. And you can even forget God. It takes a lot of endurance through so much pain to remember.

Today my mother was here. She appeared in a dream coming out of my bathroom, not smiling but looking pleased and supportive at what she saw here. Also today, I surrendered to God and Jack, and we all joined hands. What a day! A pivotal, life-altering day.

I went for an MRI on my right wrist (the possibility of a ruptured tendon and three ganglia). While in the waiting room, I did a mass of required paper work and sat down amid the negativity I felt and smelled to digest my book entitled *Walking with God* by James Keeley. I had already been captivated by several of the chapters mid-book because, at the suggestion of Shakti, I was in the process of ardently endeavoring to be open to the love and support of God "completely." I knew I had to face my fears but didn't know what my fears actually were or where they originated. I was about to find out. While reading and observing the activity around me, I was also watching a religious daytime TV show, a program I had been aware of but never seen. It was difficult to hear exactly what was being said because of the noise in the waiting room. But I was aware it was helpful to my search for healing: my sadness, some anger, and certainly my fears.

My name was called. Obediently I followed the technician out of the waiting room to the MRI machine area. I had to strip to my underpants and remove everything on my person (including hair bands because they revealed a trace of metal). I was a waif in the cotton pajama top, which reached my ankles. I then had to go deeper into this dungeon-like abyss to the enormous MRI machine spaceship. I lay before it with my arm extended, and the technician gave me earplugs, which – when he put them in my ears – made me claustrophobic. I was told I would need these plugs because of the vibrating sound I was about to hear. I felt sick to my stomach, I felt as though I would faint, I was panicked, and I was scared to death. I then realized not only that my wrist was going into this machine but my entire body! I opened my eyes for a second – big mistake – and relived years of living in a steel shelter during World War II and the bombings of the London Blitz. I immediately sensed when the vibration started that bombs were falling, and again I was petrified. I screamed, kicked, and made the technicians stop this awful process. I had had enough. I now knew where my fears originated: from the war. I knew immediately that God had placed me in this space so I would remember this fact of fear origination. I told the technicians this is not what my God wants for me, not realizing that in fact it was exactly what He wanted: for me to remember my fears. Wow, release. Indescribable.

My mother's spirit was with me and

supported me during this traumatic MRI experience. For the first time in 60 years, I finally knew just how much she loved me. My mother had actually protected me rather than controlled me during the war; she too was full of stuffed fear. (We put on happy faces, held ourselves erect, and whistled happy tunes so no one would suspect we were afraid; that's how we dealt with our fear in WWII). After the MRI experience and walking outside, the daylight was so much brighter, my heart was buoyant, and my step was light. Parking lots were full, but for me spaces opened up. I was experiencing God's love and comfort completely.

I called my mother "Mummy" today, which is something I hadn't done in 50 years. I now knew Mummy loved me and had protected me. I was a happy inner child this day – fearless – and it felt wonderful. In fact, it was an epiphany.

NOVEMBER 26

(I dreamed I danced with Jack, but it was different. He literally swept me off my feet with steps I had never learned, but we were in perfect harmony – flying in movement – and it was wonderful. I also dreamed that I changed the diaper of a loving baby.)

Me: I dreamed I danced with you last night. Honey, was I right?

Jack: Yes, you were.

Me: I didn't think I would ever dance with you again.

Jack: We can have it all, sweetie. God wants us to dance with him and with each other. I wanted you to be aware of this and that you will also dance again. You have been feeling a little burdened with physical pain, but it will dissolve. I'm so proud of you. You are doing so well with learning. I am always with you, always. Not a minute goes by when you are alone. I am there to support you. I am there to help you. I see the beauty of our work together (the energy channeling) and the happiness it brings you, and I am still blessed by your person. You are wonderful. God sees your work on all levels and is rewarding you with the fun you feel. The pictures of our work are magnificent. It doesn't matter what others think. It is magnificent work, so pure and full of light.

Me: What was the baby?

Jack: Our baby, our work, recently born.

Me: Shakti advised me to be open to God's love, and I feel the difference it is making.

Jack: That's what God wants and that's what I want. Just lay back while doing your work and all will be well for you.

December 1 was a really sad day for me. While cleaning the bedroom, I placed my hands inside Jack's slippers to feel the remnants of what I knew to be him. I kissed the inside of the slippers as I rubbed my hands from the toes to the heels and brought my hands to my face. I miss Jack's physical body so much. I cried and cried.

Yes, I keep his toothbrush, all the towels he used, and our shared bedsheets. Anything that had Jack's touch and fingerprints is of tremendous value to me – more than gold – for anything he ever bought me is treasured. I touch the doorknobs and light plates of areas he used, just to possibly touch him. I cannot yet eat at restaurants where we went together. The memories are fresh, and the pain is great.

It has been eight months since Jack's body ceased, and in some ways it seems like an eternity. On December 1, I stood in the kitchen with a countertop full of papers – unfinished business that will take a long time to complete – but Jack kept telling me I would have enough time to do everything. I tried to have conversations with him that day, but he doesn't talk to me when I am sad. He doesn't like that. Jack wants me happy or at least in a somewhat receptive, open state. I know it's the vibration, but it's very difficult to elevate when in grief.

Later that evening while cleaning Jack's bathroom at the base of his commode, I said to myself, "What a good thing I'm going to be with him again sometime."

Jack: You are still with me now, sweetheart.

Me: Oh, how quickly I forget.

Jack: You are still doing too much. You will have time for everything. Trust me.

(I recognized that maintaining this "trust" is not easy, yet little by little I am becoming aware that the art of listening for God's voice and obeying His direction and Will is well worth the effort. It does take effort to be happy when grieving.)

DECEMBER 10

Me: Hi, sweetheart. Are you there?

Jack: Always.

Me: I know you see what I am doing, but I want you to know I feel I am making some right choices for my life. I have met some wonderful new lady friends this year, and next year I plan to have a little celebration like I did seven years ago with old friends. But this time it will be for new friends: ladies I know who are like-minded, ladies I can grow with. I need a little network of compatible friends.

Jack: I know you do, baby, and I am delighted by your plan. You will all help each other and therefore the universe. I will always be around. You can depend on that.

Me: I am working with Ritchie, Shakti, and Robin (a new friend), and my body seems to be healing – no medicines, no surgeries for me except maybe later my stubborn toe. Maybe my stubbornness is what robs me of my energy. I so want my body and my mind to be healed. You see how I try. Lend a hand whenever you can.

Jack: I support you; know that. I send strength; know that. You are never alone; know that.

Me: Don't forget our friend Amber Fortune's cat, **Gwen**. I thought you said last night that she's hidden somewhere in the neighborhood. Can you help direct **Gwen** to the new house Amber has recently moved to? I know how dogs want their owners, but cats want their familiar space. I was so glad you built the *Cat House* for our cats when we first moved here. It was so important.

Jack: I still feel Gwen is hunkered down some place fairly close by. I am standing by to work with you on whatever you tell me.

Me: We are unique in our abilities together. It makes me happy.

Jack: Me too. God is ready to support us, so we can do no wrong.

DECEMBER 12

Me: You are there. I know now.

Jack: Yes, sweetie, always standing by for you

when you are ready for me.

Me: I think I'm starting to come out of the doldrums. I hope almost every tear I have for you has been shed. The love grows and grows, but the tears are beginning to cease.

Jack: I am so relieved because I see how that weakens your body and your vibration. Keep up the vibration because that's what allows us to communicate. I love the communication as much as you do.

Me: It is raining today and cold, but it is winter and to be expected; not many cats going out today, and you know they don't like that very much.

Jack: Do what is the best for you to keep the workload manageable.

Me: The lovely ladies I mentioned yesterday are all very spiritual and different from anybody I have known. We seem to have that deep connection of understanding of our higher purpose, and that is what I have been looking for because that's where I can feel myself growing. They all seem to understand what you and I are doing. As I said before, I intend to pursue these friendships.

Jack: That is what I want for you too. Do whatever you have to for this level of growth. It is so important; in fact, it is everything right now. The world may not be safe, but remember you always are.

Me: I have seen butterflies this week, yellow and multicolored. Is it you?

Jack: Yes. I make myself visible from time to time because I know it lifts your spirit. I am so very proud of you and your endeavors. How you handled the troublesome neighbor (who was invasive to our property) with such open arms and heart was momentous in your growth. Like Audrey said, "You met the devil head on and broke his shell." You are a joy to watch.

DECEMBER 15

(I caressed Jack's bed pillow and kissed his picture that I sleep with.)

Me: Do you see me when I kiss your pictures?

Jack: Yes I do, and I feel flattered by the ways you honor me.

Me: I love you more now than I ever did.

Jack: You are able to because you have cleared so many of your fears. It is all so good, and I am oh so proud.

Me: My assistant walked out today. She said she couldn't work for me any longer. I was just a little surprised because you said she would be here until the end. I laugh now and think you must have meant the end of the week.

Jack: She has many problems that don't relate to you or to me. She has a lot of work to do on herself.

Me: I felt very little loss because I recognized I was spending so much of my time counseling her moods.

Jack: You have let her go with dignity on your part, and that is commendable. As I always say, "The right ones are coming." There may be several, but they all come for a reason: to teach you or to learn themselves. Have no fears; our book will be.

Me: Our energy channeling brings me great joy. And according to Kay and Audrey, it is a very special gift we have together, and we could not do this work were you not where you are. Kay dictated a lengthy outline of what all this means, and Audrey transcribed it along with pictures of the colorings I did of what you enabled me to see. She sent this to 50 of her spiritual friends and is now getting feedback as to the pure healing power of the drawings. For me it is difficult to believe when I look at these unusual but colorful pictures. We have apparently only just begun what we have been able to do in many lifetimes before.

Jack: Yes, my love. We are working partners who will make a small impression on the earth plane. What a blessing it is to be together again.

Me: Apparently with your newfound revitalized powers, you hold down the earth so that the light can come in. I work with you to bring it in. It makes me very happy to know what is happening and that it is happening through you. You are allowing God's light and love to come through. It is oh so wonderful, and I feel the blessing of it all. Kay said in her reading that you will never leave me, and that's all I need to know. You know you have my heart, and I know you will never leave me. We both have what we want from each other. THANK YOU GOD. I have more than divine sufficiency. I overflow with goodness and blessings. I have it all. Divine order prevails. I love you, Jack.

Jack: I know, sweetie, and I love you too. You serve God and me and the universe well.

Me: What about Amber's kitty *Gwen*?

Jack: I don't see her here. I think someone else is feeding her, but she's not happy. Amber needs to keep the energy high for wanting her return.

Me: I am told by Kay I have the gift of healing energy in my hands. Can you help my right hand to heal so that I don't have to wear this brace to support my wrist?

Jack: I have told you: a little more rest and it will dissolve.

LATER THAT DAY
(I was cleaning and kissing Jack's pictures.)
Me: Again, do you feel me when I kiss your pictures?
Jack: Yes. I feel and see anything and everything you do to honor me. I thank and bless you every time. You are perfect.

DECEMBER 16
Me: The time I spend with you is the most rewarding. I love the cats, I love the land, and I love our new channeling work; but mostly I just love to sit and talk to you, almost about nothing, just like we always did. I'm going to the office now to do book work. Tomorrow I have two men coming to pick up where my assistant left off with the writing of our book. What do you think?
Jack: The more mature one could certainly do the work, but whether or not he would want to will remain to be seen. He is quality.
Me: I don't have to tell you how things are; you know. But **Ching** is doing so well, probably the healthiest cat on the land. I take excellent care of her. She hardly ever misses a meal. She is there like clockwork, morning and night.
Jack: Yes, I know, but take excellent care of yourself.
Me: God, I miss him.
GOD: HE IS THERE. YOU JUST HAVE TO THINK ABOUT HIM DIFFERENTLY. YOUR WORK IS DIFFERENT. YOUR MISSION IS DIFFERENT.

CHRISTMAS EVE

Me: Sweetheart, are you there on Christmas Eve?

Jack: I never leave your side. I see you surrender to God's hands, and I am happy. You are healed. Have no doubt about it. You needed a slowdown message, and this was it. You are doing well. I am mighty proud of your growth. I always told you it would get better and better for us, and it will. You have healing power in your beautiful hands, and when I join you -- as with everything we did together -- it will be miraculous.

Me: I tried to light a candle for you this morning, but I couldn't.

Jack: You don't need to. Light it for yourself. Do everything for yourself. Remember now where I am and how happy I am. My only wish is for you to be happy too. Do whatever you need. I will be waiting when the time comes and your work on earth is complete.

CHRISTMAS DAY

Me: It feels wonderful to honor the birth of Jesus Christ and know completely that this is what the day is all about. This year I did not accept any of the commercialism of the holiday season, and it felt so good. I gave things of mine that I felt others would enjoy. Today has been a day of soul searching as you well know, and I feel I have learned a lesson from **Ching**. **Ching** trusts us completely. We love her without conditions and provide everything she could possibly wish for. She knows we will be there morning and night. We – and now I – never let her down no matter what the weather or circumstances. It is a delicious feeling to be trusted. I feel like God must feel when we trust him. I plan to start giving

God more pleasure starting this very day. I know you are happy to hear this.

Jack: That's for sure, sweetie. God loves you even more than I do, and he will never let you down. You have said many times, "He is in charge and all is well." I can see you have had a blessed day, counting your blessings and refining your spirit. Good girl. You are so loved. The path you are taking is leading you right into God's arms. Your needs will forever be met.

Audrey called me on Christmas Day and said that she had a message for me from Jack. She read it to me over the phone:

Hello Sweetie --
We are doing the most marvelous work together, and it is only the beginning. You have no idea the areas and coverage it will have. The world will be as a dot, for there is where our love and healing will go. The vibration is so high; only those worthy shall receive and know of the change.
You have done most well today, and I have been near in thought and presence. The cats sense me, as do you. **CAT HAVEN** *is protected, my dearest, and all is at peace. I am most proud of you. Together we are One!!*
                                        Jack

While talking to Audrey, I told her I was undecided as to what to call the book. She recommended that I ask Jack.

Me: What should we call our book, honey?

Jack: Conversations with me; I'M STILL HERE!

JANUARY 4, 2008

Me: Good morning, sweetheart. I know you're here. I don't have to ask. I'm starting to feel your presence now.

Jack: Yes, I am. It is a new year, and I want it to be good for you. I continue to watch your progress and see clearly your growth and willingness to reach for the light.

Me: I so want to feel God's love, but I too see clearly that I get myself in the way sometimes with programmed fears and not being able to do the work because of physical ailments such as my hand, my foot, and also limited food selections right now. I truly do my best to follow the advice of those who know what is best for me, but it is not easy and not comfortable.

Jack: By spring you will be feeling different and better. You worked so hard for six months, and now you have had to take it easy for six months.

Me: I am very comfortable with the new young man I have working with me on the book, the land, and other projects. He seems mature and knowledgeable, which is something I have not enjoyed since you.

Jack: He is all of those things and will be loyal. His eyes are opening to a new realm of thinking.

Me: I used to feel your energy a little stronger than I do now.

Jack: That's because I hold back purposely so that you can rest your body. If I come forth, you will simply extend yourself and do more and more; and for now, that is not what you need. Rest, my love, and take it easier.

Me: You know, the love bond never stops.

Jack: I see and I feel everything. I saw Ivy last night surrender to your touch, and it made me happy. She is difficult, I know; even for me, she was temperamental. As we always said, she is a pistol.

Me: It was a very special day today. *Ivy* allowed me to pet her again this morning, and I know she felt good. I felt like God must feel when we allow him to do for us. Jack, do you see how beautiful and dependable *Ching* is? I was on the white deck yesterday with the young man who was helping type our book. It was the middle of the morning and she allowed us to see her. I think she thought it was you.

Jack: I was there too, and she probably did see me. And yes, she is remarkable.

Me: Maria comes today for a few hours and helps me so much. Also today, all the cats – including *Rose* and *Booger* (who have been trapped inside one of the buildings) – are going out. It has been freezing cold, and I managed to trap those outside cats to protect them. Today and tomorrow, it will be in the 70s. I keep thinking about this time last year when you were on South Padre Island kayaking and working; seems like yesterday, yet seems like an eternity.

Jack: I know. I still have memory, but know I am happier now than I was then. My only interest on the earth plane is your progress, and you are doing so well. Let go, baby, let go of fears and pain; and know all is in divine order. Every day is exactly as it should be. Don't fight it; accept it. See the light and feel the love of God, of me, and for yourself.

Me: Calm me – I think those words do the trick. By the way, what do you think of our new work channeling the healing energies?

Jack: It is certainly unusual in form, but don't

take time to judge the outcome. Know it does nothing but good. It may not be recognized by even the recipient, but know it is only good for the vibration.

JANUARY 12

Me: Were you here this morning to help me?

Jack: Yes, baby, I was. It hurts me to see you struggle and know how much you want the peace. You have the peace. It is yours: accept it, trust it. It is nothing you have to work for. It is yours, God's gift to you. I totally support this and bring it to you for God. Trust me, trust me, trust me. I want nothing but peace and comfort for you. My love enfolds you.

Me: Sometimes I get afraid that you will come back to the earth plane again and I will not find you.

Jack: No more, sweetheart. This is the place for me; and no matter how long it takes for you to do your work, I will be here waiting to join you again. Have no fears; we will be together for eternity. With God now, we are one. Don't forget that. Don't ever forget that.

Me: I have glimpses of pure joy when we do our work together, but in between I am having to work things out for myself. I don't know what I would do without Audrey.

Jack: You have added so much to her life, and I don't want you to forget that. She has learned so much through both of us.

Me: I am learning that our work together really does help people. Audrey's daughter, Terri Alves, gave a spectacular glowing report two nights ago on energy we channeled to her.

Jack: You bet it does. Together we have power

-- God's power -- because we are both open to receiving His love. By the way, tell Shakti her son will be well again.

Me: In the house, I feel I am getting the message through *Ivy* that you are here.

Jack: Yes, I am using her. She needs to be useful in some way to both of us. She does see me. She is a bit confused and wants comfort, so I send her to you for petting. It seems to be working. I know you are in her room this morning.

Me: Yes. You must have been around a lot this week because she has come to me quite often.

Jack: Yes, sweetie, when I see you struggling I am always around.

Me: I am reading an exquisite book Paul Minar sent to me about life in between lives, and it is like food for my soul, that's for sure. Your leaving so suddenly…was that a test for me?

Jack: Not as far as I'm aware. I had no need to test you. Maybe God had His reasons on the timing, but not me.

Me: We never had any expectations of this departure, did we? We never discussed it. We always planned to go together.

Jack: We could have talked every day about what might happen, but that would have done no good and would certainly have destroyed the good life we enjoyed. It is all God's choice, sweetheart. It was my best life ever with you. I have absolutely no regrets and don't want you to either. We were perfect together and still are. I see you petting Ivy and thank you for your newfound friendship. It makes Ivy happy, and I see the joy it brings to you.

Me: Being with you calms my soul, and I am so

very grateful I have allowed this to be. I would never be happy if we didn't maintain a connection.

Jack: Oh, my love, we are forever more connected. Remember now: I have your heart, you gave it to me, and again I made you a promise to never leave you. We are both honorable souls, so have no silly fears. Enjoy, enjoy, enjoy. Love always.

JANUARY 13

Me: The world will never know the you I grew to know.

Jack: Don't be sad, sweetie. It doesn't matter what the world knows. It only matters what you know. What a lucky guy I am to have found you. I will never leave you. Trust me. I stand beside you all the way.

Me: My body is getting better. I can see and feel it.

Jack: Yes. I witnessed that too. I told you it would dissolve once you surrendered. God is your friend, your help in every need. Stay on course. You are doing great.

JANUARY 14, 9:52 PM

Me: I love you, Jack. I so love you.

Jack: I love you too, sweetie. Don't cry. I hate to see you cry.

Me: Calm me down (instantly felt). I talked a lot to Paul Minar today about his life, his work, and his cat *Jordon*.

Jack: Tell him not to worry about his cat. This sickness won't last. Change his diet. Paul will always be a good friend for you. He's going to have a lucky year this year, and he deserves it. You don't have to worry sweetheart about a thing. You will have everything you need and by the time you join me, everything will be exactly as you want it. Others are still waiting in the wings for the right timing, and it may not all be this year. Stay happy. I love to see you happy and beautiful. Take care of yourself in every way you see fit. Be comfortable, be pain-free, and enjoy your life. We will be together when the time is right. Never think otherwise. You are for eternity my lady, and I believe I am your man.

Me: Yes you are, my sweetheart. I always want to wear my wedding ring – my special Hawaiian one – for best occasions because it is fragile, and another one for every day. I don't ever want anyone to think I'm not married. Nothing changed our marriage status. We never ran out of love, and I'm your wife forever and ever.

Jack: Good, but don't deprive yourself of another experience. It will never change what we are to each other. I just want you to have a good life.

Me: You always did. God only knows what a great husband and best friend you were to me – the best of the best. I cannot thank you enough.

Jack: You did, honey, you did. I knew we were made for each other in so many ways.

Me: I haven't heard much from our best customers since the night you transitioned.

Jack: It doesn't matter. They learned from us, and that's all that matters. It was always a fair deal in trade.

Me: I love you, honey.

Jack: I am smiling, and I love you too; always will.

JANUARY 18, 8:50 PM
Me: How am I doing on my healing?

Jack: Very well. You need a little more patience with yourself, but know you will be restored like new.

Me: I have decided that when I cry, my tears are my overflowing love for you. Then I feel better. I don't want to hold anything inside and lock myself up; better to let it out. But I have so much love for you that I didn't express, and I am sorry.

Jack: Don't be sorry, sweetheart. I always knew where your heart was. I was and still am a lucky guy to have you as my partner for eternity. I always knew I had your heart, but you couldn't express it until recently. I knew, so don't be upset at anything. As I have said before, knowing is always better than seeing. I knew.

Me: You know I am meeting these lovely ladies, and it is comforting and exciting to be aware such people exist. I'm not unhappy living alone because I like alone time to think, to be, and to relax; and it seems most of all, after the hectic days here, I need to relax.

Jack: I know, and I encourage it. Just do nothing; it is totally okay. I am right by your side, and know I am always in the room when you pet Ivy. She is difficult, but she is coming around. Patience is the only thing you lack.

Me: I have noticed winters are so cold without you. I have never disliked winter as much as this year. I cannot wait for the hummingbirds to return and the sun to shine every day.

Jack: Be the sunshine yourself. Shine your light, baby; you are so full of light.

Me: Thank you.

JANUARY 21

Me: Like you said, you are here when *Ivy* comes to me and insists I pet her.

Jack: I do that. I know it makes you feel better and starts your day well, and she certainly loves it.

Me: I continue to recognize how I simply did not understand the intensity of your affections for me when you were here on the earth plane, but I do now; better late than never.

Jack: It doesn't matter, because I felt it. It was all part of the process. I see and feel everything now and am blessed. What you now feel is not too late and is not wasted because I receive it and I get it. Nothing you do now goes unaware or unappreciated. I see it all and feel it all, and it's wonderful. Never forget, sweetie, we are and always will be spiritual beings, and the lessons go on and on here or there. There is no difference.

LATER THAT MORNING

Me: I think *Jacques* is a miracle.

(*Jacques* is a black and white, 10-year-old, outdoor cat who had had a stroke eight months ago and now happily lives in the back house portico.)

Jack: I think you are a miracle. You have loved him and cared for him so well.

JANUARY 22

(This was a most miserable night for me: vomiting, chills, nausea, the works.)

Me: Jack, why am I sick?

Jack: Too intense, trying too hard to make things right for yourself. Relax, sweetie; more time to rest and less rushing to see doctors, even though they are natural healers. You have the power to heal yourself. Let go. Let God do His work through you. Yesterday's journey was too much for you, and don't try to take in so much nutrition at one time. It becomes toxic. Rest today, all day. You can even forget the wildlife. They will be okay.

Me: *Ching* is my only concern.

Jack: Show Maria. She can do it.

LATER, 9:25 PM

Me: I don't understand that when I seem to need you the most, you are not there for me. Today has been a very painful day physically and emotionally, and I did not feel your presence at all.

Jack: You didn't allow my presence. You were so concerned with yourself.

Me: I was hurting badly. It is not the time to relax when you hurt. Vomiting every 30 minutes didn't exactly allow for relaxation. I tried very hard to let go. I read all the right literature, but I couldn't do it. I'm sorry.

Jack: Not necessary to feel sorry. You're doing very well, and Dr. Stakes is good for you and so is Vi (Dr. Stakes' nurse). You can trust Vi. She understands.

Me: I suppose it is now really time to accept what is and allow myself to be happy. I know you are, and that's great. But the old part of me feels guilty that I would do things without you.

Jack: Oh, I love you so completely and wish more than anything that you would allow yourself pleasure. You always seemed to have difficulty with that. Stop right this minute and go for all the fun you can create. I have your heart, sweetheart. What more could anyone ask? Trust me that I will be here for you when the time is right. Trust that

God wants you to be happy; you are so deserving.
Don't be afraid of anything. I mean that. Don't be
afraid. Let go. Let God take over your life. You will
not want for anything for yourself or the animals.
Let go, sweetie, let go.

JANUARY 24

Me: I know that like God, you are present everywhere. I know you see I have allowed myself to become emotionally blocked with pain at your physical absence and light from my life. I am sorry for myself and my lack of refined wisdom. It seems I'm hurting myself in some way to please you, and we agreed we would never do that. We would never hurt ourselves to please the other. So today I stop. You don't want it and neither do I. I have no idea what the next moment will bring for me, but knowing you are happy needs to be all I need. But I want to be happy too.

Jack: I want you to be happy too, my darling lady and wife. Know that is all I want for you however that comes to pass. We are still together; understand that completely. We are still together. Get well and be happy. That's all I want. Know that your happiness is mine, and go for it.

Me: Okay, I will. Our loves never dies. Our love will never cease.

Jack: That's for sure. Trust me, trust me, trust me.

LATER, 11:16 AM

An affirmation for and from Me:

NO MORE PITY POTTY FOR ME –
YOU ARE HAPPY DOING GOD'S WORK
– IN HEAVEN
I AM HAPPY DOING GOD'S WORK – ON EARTH
WHAT ELSE IS THERE?
WE ARE STILL TOGETHER –
YOU HAVE MY HEART –
YOU WILL NEVER LEAVE ME –
ALL IS WELL AND UNFOLDING AS IT SHOULD –
I KNOW GOD IS HAPPY WITH BOTH OF US.

Jack: He is indeed, honey, he is indeed.

Me: That's all there is!!! Physically my body is totally healthy. My emotions have become blocked but are releasing as of this moment. My spirit is pure – that I know – and soars with yours among our precious animals on this beautiful land.

JANUARY 25, 3:30 AM

Me: I'm sitting in your chair in your room, and it is so beautiful, so pretty. I'm blessed to have so many comforts. I can snack in the middle of the night, a perk I enjoyed when you were on South Padre Island – so small yet nice. I know you are here; I know you see the changes I am making in the house to make it MY space. I don't ever want to share this space with anyone else. It was ours; and now I am cleaning out, making it mine. You are pleased to see me pulling myself out of the muck and mire because it does no good! I want to be strong for myself as well as for you. I was strong and independent when I met you, and I want to be strong and independent again. I don't want anybody except for land and animal help. I feel the perfection of my body and that everything is dissolving as you said it would. I am so very grateful for all the traveling we did. We were great traveling companions. I have absolutely no desire to travel now; no one to help with the bags, and the world is so strange. I have everything I need. I will be all right until I join you again. I'll make the best of it, and you know that. Just stick around.

Jack: I'm here, sweetie, all the time. When you are troubled, you cannot communicate; but know I'm here. It hurts me when you doubt it, yet I understand now from a different perspective how you view things. Our relationship was perfect for me. I never doubted your love but realized your inability to always express it. As I have said before, it made every attempt on your part more special. I have no regrets about our wonderful time together. It was perfect, absolutely perfect. You are perfection to me in all ways, and I see that perfection more clearly now. It is not just a lesson for you but for me also.

THAT NIGHT

Me: It seems *Ivy* is emotionally blocked also! There were five to six piles of vomit in her room today. It's a nuisance for me and is work, but I have to sympathize. I do realize that I no longer have to wear myself out assuring you of my love for you. You know it. You know it better than I do. I guess it's my old, guilty way of trying to reassure you that I do, I did, always have, and always will.

Jack: I know. Relax. I know.

JANUARY 26, 10:43 PM

Me: Oh honey, Robin just reminded me of something I had been taught by Datha several years ago: that you and I agreed on this life experience before we incarnated this time around. Can you imagine that? I had forgotten; yet when I think of it that way, I can accept this experience better because it was an agreement we both made (Jack's seemingly early departure). You did a fantastic job here on earth preparing everything so I would be okay. The house building, the Mission, The Trust, the paper work for The Trust, our legal wills, and everything was so in order. We agreed on it. Oh, my gosh! We decided how it would be and when it would be; and we planned your departure so that we would both be happy, dancing at a favorite place to a favorite band. Wow, what creative people. We have also planned when I will join you. I am thinking about everything being our decision, and it brings comfort. When I think about OUR doing anything and everything together, I get peaceful. Thank you for fulfilling your part of our plan so perfectly. I am told you were ready to leave. Part of me wishes you had told me that afternoon, yet inside I think I already knew because you were completing so many unfinished tasks that very day. It was OUR PLAN, and right now that makes it more joyful. At the beginning of this incarnation you knew where to look for me, you knew what to expect, and that's why you went to the newspaper in Llano that special morning in June when you did. You had been expecting me. That's why I ran the ad: to put myself out there for you to find me.

Jack: You are oh so right, and I am oh so happy you have been reminded. It was our plan, nobody else's. That's why it was so easy. It seemed like a miracle, but it was our sacred plan. Our connection is permanent for all eternity.

Me: I can now see more clearly through the eyes of love, knowing it was inevitable and remains that way. You did do a remarkable job taking care of everything *for me*. Don't worry about me. Every day I see a little more clearly the divine plan – God's plan – with our participation. It reinforces my understanding that the seeming tragedies of life were agreed upon by all parties involved before reincarnation. When you understand the agreements that were made, it makes more sense. My best friend, I love you. Good night.

Jack: It is just you and me, babe. We agreed on everything.

JANUARY 27, 12:30 AM

Me: I've just learned that before souls reincarnate, they choose their bodies and they get glimpses of each other so they know what to expect when they meet again. I recognized you by your eyes, and you recognized that I would have red hair because we saw glimpses of each other before we incarnated. You had dreamed about me for years and my red hair.

THAT MORNING
(A dream)

30 SECONDS IN HEAVEN – FOR ME
It was an exquisite, lingering, exhilarating, all-encompassing kiss from a man. He did not look like Jack, but this would have been something Jack would have expressed. I had just met this man. I knew I had experienced a past life with him because of the attraction. I called him

aside and told him so. He was very simply dressed in shorts, and I think he had been smoking. His voice was husky and to me, attractive. He came close to me, and I mentioned that I knew we had known each other in another lifetime. He seemed to doubt my philosophy but leaned forward to kiss me and with a smile like Jack's, said, "I want it all," but in a friendly, crazily sweet, and funny tone. He kissed and kissed and kissed me, and it was incredible. Breathtaking. It was not the way Jack kissed unless he had learned to kiss differently. It was not sexual yet resonated dizzily from the heart. I knew I didn't want it to stop, yet I woke up.

I was on a totally different vibration. My body was elevated and pain-, sickness-, and heaviness-free. I rushed to get dressed because I saw it was late for me – 7:30 am – and Maria was coming. I then saw that she was already here. By the time I got down the long driveway, some of the heavy, physical distresses were returning. I do believe, however, I was given the opportunity to experience the heavenly realm of bliss through this kiss of someone I knew well.

A LITTLE LATER

Me: Honey, was that you?

Jack: Yes, it was. We do things differently here. It just comes naturally because of the vibration.

Me: Oh, I can't wait for that. It took all of my discomforts away.

Jack: I knew it would, and I wanted to help you. You can now think of that whenever you hurt.

157

Me: Why did you look so different?

Jack: It was how I looked to you in another lifetime.

Me: I love both of your appearances.

Jack: Of course you would. You loved me no matter the color of my skin. Love is love. We could both have been different skin colors, and it would have been wonderful.

Me: You sexy thing, still keeping me attracted to you; not that anything has faded, but I think that was smart.

Jack: As I always told you, it only gets better.

Me: That's just like you, honey, that's just like you.

Jack: Because I am still me -- the me you love you have known for so long -- I just wanted to share heaven with you.

Me: I'm so glad you did and that it was YOU.

Jack: Your dreams will always be me.

Me: I am grateful to have you with me. I'm going to share this experience. People need to know the good things they have in store for them. It was out of this world.

Jack (laughing): It sure was.

20 MINUTES LATER

(I laughed, and I kissed one of my favorite pictures of Jack taken and located at the front door. It had been taken before we had gone dancing one night, and he was posing the way he liked me to pose.)

Me: Thank you, thank you, thank you. WE have something so special. I want the world to know about it.

Jack: Baby, they will. You write it and they will come to buy it. Guaranteed.

Me: You are giving me this book.

Jack: You bet. I am doing it for our babies.

Me (laughing joyfully): You are feeding me this book from heaven, and I don't have any doubt that you are here now.

FOUR HOURS LATER

Me: I still feel spellbound like nothing will ever harm me.

Jack: It won't, my lady, it won't.

Me: I feel enveloped in light like I am open to receiving and radiating. It is indescribably delicious.

Jack: We always had fun sharing, and it continues. I am having fun watching you. Remember I told you I was with God and there was nothing like it? Now you have a taste of what I was talking about. Earthly pleasures pale in comparison.

Me: They sure do. A lot of my fears have been dispelled by 30 seconds in heaven. Thank you, sweetie, for changing the course of my life yet again. I feel like a little kid with a big secret that I am bursting to tell the world.

Jack: Oh you can, honey, you can. There are so many hearts open to this knowledge and comfort. Don't doubt the power in which we share.

Me: Good conversation today.

Jack: For sure. You are with me. Your vibration is good. I appreciate that, for there is so much to share.

6 PM

Me: Upon reflection, I believe today was the happiest day of my entire life. No day was ever as joy-filled even when you were here physically. For me, it was happier than coming to America, happier than any wedding day – even with you, Jack – happier than any exotic vacation and I enjoyed quite a few. This day's joy surpasses all other days spent with you. You sure know what you are doing having me experience a glimpse of heaven. I can now fly. May I live every day like today. One long, lingering, sizzling, vibrating, warm, ecstatic kiss – that's how heaven felt to me. Thank you for the healing.

Jack: God does it all. God does it all, baby.

11 PM

Me: I have just read more of my favorite book, *Destiny of Souls*, where it is confirmed that you and I are primary soulmates, Eternal Partners. We caught glimpses of each other before we incarnated. Your brown eyes and my red hair allowed us to recognize ourselves. I am learning so much every day, and the book Paul sent me is of such interest. No one and nothing can turn off our love. Isn't that delicious? Ooh, what comfort it brings me to think of eternal love. Nothing will ever keep us apart. I finally understand you so much better. When you would say, *"Come back to bed,"* it was just your need to be close, and there was never a threat for me.

JANUARY 28

Me: Strange day for me. I gave my whole support to Jane and Dwight Hume (old friends) but could not control the anguish it brought me. I think I am realizing something like their experience (Dwight had been hospitalized with life threatening internal injuries) could have happened to us, and I would have had to take care of you. I certainly would have, but our animals and Our Mission would have been totally off course.

Jack: That's for sure, baby. Everything happens exactly as it should. Your life has changed more than enough, as will theirs. There are lessons for all of us in what happens. God knows what he's doing.

Me: I could not have borne the pain of seeing you hooked up to machines.

Jack: That was not the plan for us. You had absolutely too much to care for without me. Your adjustments have taken major time and energy. You are learning your lessons, and they are learning theirs. The projection is just different.

Me: I recognized when I was 11 years old that I wanted to be healthy and take care of myself: no cigarettes, no beer. I am a bore, but I have enough other manifestations of distress to cope with.

Jack: You do, and you are mastering over all. Relax, honey. Find a teacher of yoga or a class. This is what you need. You will meet like-minded people. Start searching. I like your new gloves (for the stress injury). Get more. I think they will benefit you.

Me: I didn't know you would notice such a small thing.

Jack: If it helps you, I notice. Pull back your energy for yourself.

Me: Do I still look beautiful to you? They say the loss of your love ages you 10 years, which means I'm 82.

Jack: No way. You are still 52 to me and a ravishing beauty. You will always, always be beautiful to me. By the way, remember: we didn't plan to be hooked up to machines. We planned to go out dancing.

161

Me: If I am dancing with another man, will that be okay with you?

Jack: You know I was never jealous. Just come to me but not until you are ready. Take care of our business before you do. Everything at **CAT HAVEN** *is important to me too. Everything is as it should be for everyone.*

Me: Everybody seems to be doing well at **CAT HAVEN**. The resilience and perseverance of the cats is incredible – shining examples of how to behave. *Morgan* defies belief, and *Rory* (who has diabetes) is magnificent. Tomorrow *Morgan* goes to the vet, and I will have my helpmate take me. I cannot carry her anymore, especially in a cage. She is mighty heavy. I love to stay talking to you; it's truly like you never left.

Jack: Baby, I have never left your side. Working, driving, shopping...I am there with you and always happy when you do things for yourself.

Me: I love you, Jack, and we will talk tomorrow. Right now I'm going to see Connie (a dermatologist) for a spot I had on my chin that has almost gone away.

Jack: I told you everything would dissolve. Trust me, sweetie, trust me. I know what's happening. I see everything clearly.

JANUARY 29

I was in Dr. Stakes' office and was the only patient in the waiting room. Music was playing: "Your kiss, your kiss, I miss your kiss..."

LATER

I decided to have a celebratory dinner at a Chinese buffet because my chin had healed. The fortune cookie at the end of the meal stated, "You will become an accomplished writer." Let's hope so!

JANUARY 31, 10:10 PM

Me: I know you know that just because I don't come into your room and sit in your chair doesn't mean I'm not thinking about you.

Jack: Of course I do. We are together at all times and in all places. There is no separation.

Me: This morning I was able to give away some of your dinner shirts to my helpmate. He seems appreciative.

Jack: Yes, baby, he is. He is one of the right ones you waited patiently for. He has much to give to you and others.

Me: Sometimes this reality is difficult to grow into, and I want to cry and cry with sadness.

Jack: Oh no, sweetie, don't be sad. Why would you allow that? We are both together doing God's will, and there is nothing more. Remember the joy you felt when I kissed you?

Me: Your beautiful face, your beautiful eyes, your beautiful body, and those incredible hands...

Jack: They surround you and have for lifetimes and will forever. When you reach for me, I am there. What you feel is real. You know my touch as I know yours. Always knowing is the best. It is sacred and secret and ours to share. I know you, I love you, and I am there.

Me: You are the best – so comforting – and you always were.

Jack: I always will be, for you.

Me: Yes, my man.

Jack: Yes, my lady. Shine your light for all to see.

FEBRUARY 1

Me: Last night I was reading about animal and pet spirits. It seems in heaven we have to go find their spirits, and I know you have done this for me.

Jack: Yes, I certainly have. Our pets are our children.

Me: This morning I distinctly heard **Pardy** give one long, strong bark on the back deck to wake me up the way he used to. Did you tell him to do this?

Jack: For sure. I knew it would make you happy to hear him again.

Me: When you told me earlier last year you caught **Lady** and **Butch's** spirit and that of the bird, is that because you were watching our place?

Jack: You bet. I know what is going on and stay ready to greet our family at all times.

Me: That is so nice to know, and it is so incredible that from this new dimension you continue to do things you know will make me happy. You prove to me over and over again of your presence in my life. You are still here. You see. You listen. And you bring forth some unique and pleasant surprises to me. Thank you.

Jack: Don't cry. This is my joy to be with you and to please you. Remember, you gave me your heart and when it is heavy or hurting, I feel that and want to help. Over here we all want to help. Unless you are in contact with us as you are, families think it is miraculous when surprises happen, but we know they are hurting and do our best to help out. It is a continuous journey, and we are all in it together.

(I thought I then understood Jack to say, *"Nothing stops love, and lessons continue. It is only awareness that changes."*)

Me: I just want to stay in your chair and be with you.

Jack: You are always with me, but the sitting is something I approve of.

FEBRUARY 3

    I had my first glimpse in 2008 of what I believe to be Jack's spirit outside the front gate. I was standing on the ladder my friend and helper Ray Rogers held for me. While I returned to a vase on top of the mailbox some of the silk flowers the wind had blown around, I saw a beautiful, bold, yellow butterfly. In February butterflies are rare, but then again so is Jack.

> "For instance, souls can become rocks to capture the essence of density, trees for serenity, water for a flowing cohesiveness, *butterflies for freedom and beauty* and whales for power and immensity. People deny these actions represent earthly transmigrations. I have also learned souls may become amorphous without substance or texture and totally integrate into a particular feeling, such as compassion, to sharpen their sensitivity."
> –from *Journey of Souls* by Michael Newton, PH.D.

FEBRUARY 7

Me: Since I know you are always near, I don't have to write every day. We talk, and that is all I need. However, today I was connecting with Jane Hume in Santa Fe regarding the status of our friend and her husband Dwight. Miracles are happening for her, and she certainly deserves them. Dwight has been very sick and continues to hurt, but he is so brave.

Jack: He is indeed. They have a remarkable relationship like ours, yet I believe the reason he lingers is so that both of them can finish what they decided to do in this lifetime. It is a partnership of learning, not for either one separately. I will stand by him in his time of need. You too deserve miracles, my beloved, and they will never cease for you. I can see that you are seeking the right kinds of support for your health issues. Keep it natural and you will be like new before too long. You are so loved by God and by me.

FEBRUARY 8, 6:41 AM

Me: Good morning, God.

GOD: GOOD MORNING, MY CHILD.

Me: Good morning, Jack.

Jack: Good morning, my lady.

Me: It is still dark outside and only 38 degrees, so I thought I would warm my heart and spend a few minutes with you.

Jack: Glad to be of help. I love to help you in any way I can, but remember now: you are in charge of yourself and can help yourself by trusting just a little bit more. Don't waste energy on worry, sweetie. Just lay back and trust. You have the power. You have the power you need. You are learning to know all is well for you. God will never let you down and neither will I. It is your faith that is being tested. Do you believe God can help you, or do you believe you have to do it all yourself? All you need is more faith.

Me: Thank you. I know better. I am so grateful for the happy life you shared with me. I declare myself your spirit wife. When you've had the best, that's all you need, and you are the best for me.

Jack: I appreciate that, but I want you to enjoy every experience life brings you. It doesn't change us, but enjoy, my lady, enjoy.

Me: Once again, your unselfish nature comes through. I know it is you. What a love you are.

Jack: You too, baby, you too.

FEBRUARY 9

Me: I am stuck – stuck in muck and mire again today – but I am not embarrassed to tell you. The pain of missing your beautiful physical form and strength is debilitating at times. For several weeks now, I have inflicted suffering on myself. I know it all. I know the eternity of this process, but I am stuck on you. As I walk down the driveway and see the beauty of this place and as I feed the gorgeous animals in **CAT HAVEN**, I recognize fully how much you gave me, God gave us, and how lucky I am. But I still MISS YOU. I need some help. What you thought I could do last June on my birthday, I am still struggling with. It was time to move on, you said. I'm not there yet.

Jack: I see that, baby. I see that clearly. It hurts me too.

Me: We are both doing God's will: you in heaven and me on earth. I'm glad it's me here on earth. It is obvious I need to be here because I've more lessons to learn. I wouldn't want you to experience this although maybe you did if I perhaps left you first in our last lifetime.

FEBRUARY 12, 2 PM

Me: Finding a happy thing to do alone is so

difficult.

Jack: Baby, you are not alone.

Me: Are you with me all the time?

Jack: Yes, I am.

Me: But don't you have God's work to do?

Jack: Yes, I do, but I can do it all.

Me: Wow.

5 PM

Me: Is Dwight Hume on your side?

Jack: Yes, he is, sweetheart. He came over on Sunday.

Me: I have called Jane several times, but she has not responded.

Jack: She has much on her mind, as well you know.

Me: Did you greet Dwight?

Jack: Yes, along with many others. He is a very popular man.

7:30 PM

Me: Jane just called. Dwight is still here walking and talking about dreams he had and seeing himself, his son, and Jane – "a golden triage."

FEBRUARY 13

Me: I called Paul's intuitive friend Isabel Zacardi, and she told me Dwight did come over to your side and went to a healing temple for a brief time. Thus, when Jane tells me he is back here on his feet talking and accepting his circumstances, I can see how that happened. Perhaps his lesson was acceptance. It certainly seems to be mine.

Jack: More like trust for you. Trust God, baby; He is ALL MIGHTY.

LATER

I talked to Isabel, and she told me Jack is a most high teacher and would not be able to communicate with such force if he was not far along on the spiritual path himself. Isabel also said that when Jack and I were both created, God gave my hand to Jack. He is with me all the time, and I am richly blessed to have this man.

FEBRUARY 14, VALENTINE'S DAY

There were flowers in my mailbox from Mary Lee Brand, our neighbor from across the street – a most thoughtful gesture.

February 15-18 was a blur – an angry blur – with so much to do. *Minnie* was missing, and *Mr. Peaches* (the long-haired, peach-colored male cat living in the *Barracks*) was back and forth to the vet. I felt angry, a screaming mimi. I had so much responsibility and couldn't even find the time or right energy to talk to Jack. (This happened frequently. When my emotions were roaring, I could not communicate with my love.)

FEBRUARY 16

Me: It's raining, which is good. After all the rain we had last year, we have not had very much in your new rain gauge. This morning it measured one inch. I love the rain gauge. I see you everywhere, but I see you especially there. We have some sick babies today. *Mr. Peaches* needs help. He has some very unusual sores all over his head. Dr. Stried doesn't know what is causing it. Can you shed some light?
Jack: Allergy.
Me: To what?

Jack: Food.

Me: I'm not feeling you.

Jack: Your vibration is very low today.

Me: You may not feel me, but I know you are here; and if you could just lend a hand with **Mr. Peaches** and also **Minnie**, who has not come to eat for several days now…I am putting both of them in God's hands and yours. I cannot worry anymore. It is pulling me down.

FEBRUARY 20

Me: I had a crazy, mixed-up dream about all my life's happenings. I am certainly not my sweet, loving, light-filled self. I feel void of light, love, and support of you and want to get back on track. I need help. Are you still there? I haven't felt your presence in days.

Jack: Of course I am, but I cannot reach you in your pain. You just have yourself in the way, sweetie, and I cannot come through to you.

Me: I don't know how to be the way I am right now. I need my masterful companion. I'm angry at you for leaving me with so much responsibility.

Jack: Like Mother Teresa, God trusts you completely. You are a Mother Teresa of the animal kingdom, and He trusts you so much. Everything is in divine order, I promise you. Mr. Peaches has not decided yet on what to do, but God and -- as Audrey says -- the "animal elves" are looking over him. You do your best always, and there is nothing more you can do. You gave Dr. Stried permission to do anything he could, and his hands are the best earthly hands to be in. Peaches is a champion. He is very proud of how he looks, and right now his pride is being tested. Your love helps him a lot.

Go see him today. Minnie is not ready either to leave the earth plane. She does love you but never learned to trust anyone. Keep doing all you do and sending her your loving light. She knows you love her. She really knows. That's why you keep finding her at the front door.

Me: I've been so angry with you, and now I feel shame.

Jack: Oh, honey, don't do that. I can take it. I watch you with sorrow but understanding. Your intention is so pure, and I see how you neglect yourself for the animals. Don't do that. You do come first because without you, no animal gets care; you first and then them. You are healing even though this time seems dark. I will help you shine your light today.

Me: I need your help every day.

Jack: I am here, but you don't allow me to help. Your emotions overshadow the light. Stop, stop, stop. You are only hurting yourself. Remember, the muck and mire doesn't help. Get out of it and have some fun.

Me: At least we are talking, and that makes me feel better.

Jack: I never left your side, but you were blinded by the darkness.

FEBRUARY 21, 5:16 AM

Me: Well, I know for sure that when our babies are sick, I become sick too. They are my life now. I don't need to dance; I don't need to go places. Everything I have worked for and love is right here on this land. I feel safe and close to you here. The outside (the gate) world holds nothing for me anymore. I have everything right where we live. Our creation is so perfect, a small paradise. I am blessed to have so much that we built together. You know only too well that **Mr. Peaches** came home yesterday, and he is on his way to recovering. Dr. Stried is a miracle worker with the animal kingdom. There is no doubt about that. **Mr. Peaches** recognized it yesterday and I think showed his love and appreciation in the exam room on the table when he rubbed up against Dr. Stried's healing hands and arms. **Mr. Peaches** was like a well-trained child, and I was proud of his affection toward the doctor. My feelings were the same. **Minnie** comes to the door on her own now – when all the other cats are out of the way – and tells me she's ready to eat. I think she cleaned the plate four times yesterday; just small portions, but she ate and ingested her medicine (for arthritis). What a relief! **Hamlet** came in a few minutes ago, so the day has a good beginning. Are you here this morning?

Jack: Of course. I see it all, sweetie. I just can't reach you when you put up such barriers. I don't blame you but want you to know we cannot connect during these times. I promised I would never leave you, and I never do. The shoe salesman you met yesterday allowed you to open and reflect your light. He was the instrument God used to open you to your own radiance. You could not see his light if you didn't have light. That was a good connection for you.

Me: I feel I am back on track.

Jack: You are how you should be. All is well.

FEBRUARY 23, 9:05 AM
Me: Are you with me?
Jack: I never leave you.

Me: I am such a doofus, and you cannot deny it. I never quite understood whenever I came to you with a kiss or a hug how thrilled you were, and I believe you hungered for that action on my part.

Jack: Oh I did, sweetheart, how I did. The intimacy that you always misinterpreted…but it was okay because I had you by my side. Yes, we had earthly unions, but I knew I had you spiritually also. I was a happy guy. Don't cry, baby, please don't cry. I know I have you completely. I know it, and all is well.

Me: It is the regrets that just tear me apart.

Jack: No, no, no. That is not to be. The relationship was always, always more than a physical touch and kiss, wonderful though they were. That heart connection that can never be denied was ours and will be forever more: the sharing and the caring for each other and whatever we did together. God is pleased with us.

Me: I just want to tell the world that when you have found love, don't waste a minute of any day without feeling those connections because the pain of regret is debilitating. Now I have this connection where the cats are concerned. I think I have always gone out of my way to give them everything. The thought (not to waste a single second) is more prevalent since my lessons through you. The cats can be a nuisance and they can be demanding, but I extend myself in whatever way I can to make them happy. I hope I made you happy.

Jack: Of course you did. Doubts are silly. Don't go there.

Me: I could have been so much better.

Jack: Baby, you have learned the lesson and are aware of the process. You are perfect, just plain perfect, to me.

Me: The simplest things I could've done but didn't do to make you happy…

Jack: But you did so many things that did truly improve and complete me. I was totally satisfied with you. You opened my eyes to so many things. We were partners, baby. We were equal partners.

Me: You know we never had a fight, never.

Jack: Those feelings did not exist between us this time around; maybe in other lives, but we had worked all of that out. This time was BLISS.

Me: This level of euphoria must be unique.

Jack: It happens, but I am so glad we experienced it, and it will continue to only get better. <u>The togetherness that we now have is what makes it unique.</u>

LATER

I was going to see Diane Swinney, our CPA, to give the information on our 2007 taxes. As I drove away from the gate of the property, for some reason I said to Jack, "You can take control of my car if you want to." (If you remember, he had done this a few days after his transition as well.) That was all I said. It was 12:20 pm, and I was barely going to make what I thought was a 45-minute trip to Diane's office. I felt I was running a little bit late and was stressed. The next time I had a conscious thought other than the traffic and traffic lights, I recognized I was on a freeway that I had not intended to take. I felt like I was on the wrong road, thought I was going to be really late, and panicked. How was I going to turn myself around and go back to where I thought I should have been? I continued on the freeway because the traffic was heavy. Suddenly, I saw the name of the street on which Diane's office is located. I couldn't believe it. I was on the right road at the right time; in fact, when I drove up to Diane's office, I was 20 minutes early. This trip had only taken me 20 minutes instead of the 45 I had allowed from past experience when I always took the same route. But I had let Jack be in charge and he had me to the appointment early!

After the meeting with Diane, I stayed in the driveway outside the office and told Jack he could again take charge of the wheel. I then told him I wanted to go to a particular PetSmart because shopping for the animals was next on my schedule. I did nothing but steer. I went down streets I had never considered before, with my hands on the wheel while watching the lights and traffic flow. The next thing I knew, I was outside PetSmart. I was conscious that I had made turns that would not have been my choice, but there I was at my destination. It was Saturday, and the parking lot was full with additional traffic for a pet adoption day. But to my surprise, there was one parking space just across from the entrance, and this is where Jack took my car. I started to cry with joy, and Jack said, ***"Don't cry, baby. Just have fun with me!"***

Jack was in control, getting me to the next two places I needed to go. I had to get the oil changed in my car and told the mechanics that I felt the wheels were out of balance. They found a nail embedded in the front left tire, which they could not repair. So I had to change directions and take my car to a place where Jack had a lifetime tire repair warranty. This was a diversion from my originally planned list of places to go, but Jack got me to the destination smoothly and quickly. By this time, I was in a completely different area of town from the fast food restaurant where I wanted to stop for a salad. I sort of said "hey ho" as I continued to let Jack be in charge of the driving. We made a left turn off the freeway, and there before my eyes was a brand new Jack In The Box restaurant. I was laughing by this time, and I repeatedly heard Jack say, ***"Just trust me, honey, just trust me."*** Wow. I decided from this point forward to place Jack in charge of my travels. It was a wonderful Saturday – so different from the previous one when I had been so full of anger.

LATER THAT DAY
Me: Thank you for the invitation to have fun with you. It worked.

MARCH 15, 9:32 AM
(A dream)

I seemed to be in a very tall skyscraper elevator with Jack, and we went right to the top. At the top, he went around on the side and I stayed close to the middle because I am afraid of heights. We lingered awhile. The view was incredible. Just where we entered to descend, there was a huge sort of hand washtub filled with gorgeous jewelry. The water was very sparkly and clean. I was obviously tempted and picked up as much of the jewelry as I could (almost all of it) and tried to put it in my left pocket. Some of it I wanted to keep but decided not to, so I returned everything but one pearl drop ruby. I then rode down the elevator (only me this time). When I arrived at the bottom of the building, I went to find the owner to report my findings. I found a lady who introduced me to the owner – a Donald Trump type. There was enthusiasm about the discovery, and I cannot remember if it was the lady or the man who wanted to take me further into the building to help with something decorative.

Me: Jack, does this dream have meaning?

Jack: Yes, baby, it does. Last night you came up to be with me for awhile. We took the elevator together. You still have some fears and therefore chose to remain where you did. You were tempted by all the beauty that is here and understandably wanted to take some of it with you. You knew to return it, but you were allowed to keep the ruby. It is yours. You have earned it, and there will be more beautiful things yet to come for you.

Me: Was it God? But who was the lady?

Jack: Your spirit guide.

Me: Do you know her name so I can call on her?

Jack: Tanna. She was my guide also.

Me: You know how busy I am and that sitting down to spend time with you has been difficult.

Jack: You don't ever worry about that. I am with you all the time and know how well and how much you are doing.

Me: Lou Eberle (carpenter and friend) said he saw your smiling face on Wednesday morning. That was so nice of you.

Jack: Oh, it was a pleasure. I knew he was coming to see you even before you told me that morning. I just wanted to let him know I appreciate his dedication to you and Our Mission. He is a very good man.

Me: I received the business card of a landscaping contractor on the mailbox this week. If he seems reliable, I may hire him to do the heavy landscaping that I did last year.

Jack: I wish you would. If it is not him, the right one will come. You don't have to go looking; he will come to you.

MARCH 20

The second digital thermography screening result arrived in the mail today. I promptly took it to Dr. Stakes who took time from his very busy day (the waiting room was full and I didn't have an appointment) to review the results and put my mind at rest.

Jack: Honey, God may give you a slowdown, but he will never take you away from the Mission.

LATER

(I was standing at the kitchen window looking outside and saw a beautiful butterfly.)

Me: Is that you, sweetheart? I kind of prefer thinking of you as being in the house with me.

Jack: I am everywhere.

MARCH 21 (GOOD FRIDAY)

Me: Are you there, sweetheart?

Jack: Always for you, always.

Me: You know what has been going on this week and my struggles through my fears and hopefully letting them go.

Jack: I do indeed, and you are doing a good job of releasing. I see your pain and I hold you, but you don't feel me.

Me: You know I talked with our friend Datha last

night. She's wonderful and has had pain of her own. I wish I could help.

Jack: You do when she sees your strengths. Not everyone she counsels has so much to give back. She sees your growth over the years and the effort you have put forth to achieve it. She feels comforted knowing she was part of your growth.

Me: She says you want me to get on with my life and live more in this earthly world and not so much with you. I interpreted that to mean you didn't want to talk to me.

Jack: No, sweetie, oh no. Not so. I want everything for you. You are still on the earth plane and need to take advantage of what it has to offer you – and that is much. But I am always here to add comfort and pleasure if I can. Like I told you yesterday, I am everywhere so I want you to be everywhere. You will always have me. Nothing changes that. Eternity is a meaningful word. We are partners for eternity no matter what comes in between. Right now you have your work and I have my work, but we still also work together. Our love never dies. My pleasure on the earth plane is you. God's will and yours are one, and that is what I want too.

Me: The deprivation of not talking to you would totally destroy me. That's what keeps me going on and fulfilling the work here. I would not be on this desirable path had I not met you this time around. I see the divinity of it all and your destiny with me. Thank you for showing me mine and setting everything up so beautifully for me. Remember how you would always make suggestions about doing this and building that, and then we would laugh at the enormous amount of work you created for yourself? You never really seemed to have objections, but to me you appeared to be content with what you were doing. Well, obviously those suggestions came from God through you to direct me on my path to fulfillment. I see the plan now more than ever. It was all God's plan how we met and what we did – mostly what YOU did for me; blessings, more blessings than I could have imagined. This thing we call love is oh so powerful. It tears you apart yet holds you together. I love you, Jack, more than ever. I am absolutely turned inside out with love and gratitude to God for giving me you and to you for giving so much to me and doing so much. I see it was your purpose so that I could nurture the earth plane in some small way on this special land for all these magnificent animals. You said compassion is my greatest virtue, and I have the opportunity to use it. Nurturing the earth realm is truly what I love doing most. By the way, hummingbirds are back. One arrived early on the 7th; several were here by the 19th. Now when I feed them, I have the experience of being buzzed by hummingbirds. The first one I saw I named *Kingfisher* because of his remarkable coloring and the firm band around his neck. But when I think about it, maybe it is *Sentry* (a hummingbird from the year before) who is all grown up.

Jack: Yes, I think so too. I am happy for you to know the feeling of them buzzing around your head. It is great. They are so smart to travel so far to the same locations. To hear this makes me happy too. Hummingbirds are one of my favorite birds, as well you know.

Me: Yes. You taught me about them because until you, I really didn't know very much. You are the sweetest guy I've ever met, a gentle giant for sure.

MARCH 26

Me: The last few days of our first year apart from the way we knew it have been the most painful. I want you here with me.

Jack: I am, sweetie, I PROMISE I am.

Me: You used to frequently say, *"I want you to be right next to me."* And I didn't understand the depth of that statement. Now I do.

Jack: That's all that matters, baby. Now YOU understand, and we are on the same level of understanding LOVE.

Me: I might never have arrived at this point in understanding had you not changed dimension.

Jack: That is true, but you are there now and we are both satisfied.

Me: It seems impossible, yet it is true: I love you way more than I did this time last year when you were still physically here with me.

Jack: Baby, IT ONLY GETS BETTER, and now you know that is true. You are so much more than you were, and you will continue to grow. God is pleased with your accomplishments and so am I. You cannot imagine my pride in my lady. You cannot imagine!

MARCH 30

(One year since Jack's transition)

Me: Good morning, sweetheart. This is the anniversary of my worst dream ever. Fortunately, I don't have any recollection today of anything in that realm of negativity. Mind you, I am making every resolve to forget that painful past and remember only the beautiful because there was so much that was beautiful with you and through you. I know I have learned a lot this year and my understanding of the process of this journey of life is so much deeper, but my life was enriched beyond measure through you, Jack. The book Paul gave me (about life in between lives) is of tremendous help. Did I leave any of my essence behind in the spirit world, and were you able to find it?

Jack: Yes, my love, you did, and I was immediately drawn to it for my own comfort. I think this is also what allows me the closeness to you now. It is like a sweet fragrance that I can bask in, and for me it is joyful too. I am in you, and you are in me. The connection is gripping and steadfast.

Me: I do so hope others will glean peace of mind from our continued learning together. Love never dies, just the flesh. On this earth plane in human form, we put so much effort into making the body what we think is perfect whereas we should be concentrating our efforts on molding our souls to perfection, for this is what really counts. We are oh so judgmental of the body, but never give the soul a second thought.

This has been absolutely the worst year of my life, and yet it has been the best year of my life. The lows have been so low, the highs so high; and the knowing that I am progressing in the journey of my soul is so rewarding. A good deal of credit goes to you, my most high teacher! Because of your presence, acceptance, and love of me just the way I was, your mission on earth was certainly accomplished when you first introduced me to God almost 20 years ago; and again more recently in a special dream when you stepped aside and allowed me to be blinded by the light and to feel the presence of God. I can see that God is pleased with both of us. As the ad read years ago, I am your "special lady." Now I know it is for eternity.

Jack: And I am your man.

Me: And may Almighty God continue to bless us indeed in unusual ways.

Jack: And may we shine forth his light forever in grace.

MARCH 31, 6:30 PM

(One year and one day since Jack's transition; I wanted an end for the book and wondered how it would happen.)

This time last year I couldn't see straight, stand straight, or think straight. But tonight while I was feeding *Ching* on the white deck and standing by waiting for her to finish eating, I saw a brilliantly colored monarch butterfly on Jack's and my favorite bush by the side of the deck. Of course, I spoke to it: "If it's you, Jack, come over here beside me."

Within seconds, the butterfly settled on the top of the doghouse in which *Ching* was still eating. It then flew back to the bush, returned within seconds to the doghouse, and sat on top of it. I gasped and I laughed. I extended my right hand toward the barrel, which is next to the doghouse. Before I could even take another breath, the butterfly settled in between the first two fingers of my right hand and moved around tickling the small hairs on it. Then it flew up my right arm and sat for a few seconds in the middle part. (This was a new experience for me. I had felt the finger touch of the butterfly the previous summer but not the arm.) I watched closely and talked continuously. The butterfly flew back to the bush and then over and around my head. I stood up because my neck was starting to ache, placed my body over the doghouse, and extended my right hand once again onto the barrel. Within seconds, the butterfly landed on my right forefinger for a short time. The next stopping place was my forehead and thereafter several places on my head. (It landed on my head seven times or more, and I distinctly remember counting the gentle touches.) I didn't move. I couldn't believe it. I laughed and said, "You are having fun with me, Jack." My back began to ache because of how I was positioned, and I quickly realized that **Mr. Peaches** would have to wait for his supper because nothing was going to take me from this experience. My honey was really here. I had been one year without him, and he knows I miss him.

My next position was "sitting" on the deck by the food barrel. When the butterfly settled on the outer rim of the barrel, I began conversations about how best to get our book published.

Me: Shall we get an agent?

The wings swiftly drew up tight. I interpreted this to mean: *No.*

Me: Shall we put this on the Internet?

The wings fell apart softly a couple of times. I interpreted this to mean: *Possibly.*

(My heart overflowed with love at his melodic response.)

Me: I <u>love</u> you   I <u>love</u> you   I <u>love</u> you, beyond measure.

Three times the wings unfolded slowly. My interpretation was:

I love <u>you</u>. I love <u>you</u>. I love <u>you</u>.

I then stood up and supported myself on a tree while boldly and fully extending my right arm. Within seconds, the butterfly was on my right forefinger once again, moving his head as though to talk. He positioned himself on the finger with his head facing my fingernail. I pulled my arm and hand toward my face and looked into the butterfly's eyes. Believe it or not, I attempted to kiss his wings. My breath blew him away the first time, but he quickly returned and I did the exact same thing. This time I held my breath and kissed his closed wings three times. He stayed quite still and allowed this. In between kisses he would leave for a few seconds. Just before he returned again, I kissed my hand where he had sat, and I purposely licked my finger to make it wet and relish him. When he came back, he kissed and licked my finger also, as his feet and feelers rejoiced and euphorically feasted on me. I witnessed every move, but I then recognized it was getting dark and wondered how long he would remain. I knew I was not going to be the first to leave this meeting. The last time he came to me he seemed to know it was to be the last kiss of the day because he stayed in the same place while my lips were on his elevated wings. While enraptured in this out-of-body experience with my eyes closed, I felt the whisper of his wings as he flew away.

When I arrived back at the house, it was 7:40 pm, which meant we had been together approximately one hour. I now know what Jack means when he says, *"It only gets better."* How many people on earth have kissed the wings of a live butterfly? I KNOW I will see him again, and I most certainly look forward to that next meeting.

THE END

§

MY PRAYER

LORD, HELP ME CUT LOOSE FROM THE
BONDAGE OF THINGS AND FEARS.

LET ME NOT SQUANDER MY GIFT OF LIFE ON
MY OWN SELFISH PLEASURES AND GOALS.

HELP ME TO BRING ALL MY APPETITES
UNDER YOUR CONTROL.

MAKE ME REMEMBER I AM A PILGRIM,
NOT A SETTLER.

I AM NOT YOUR FAN, BUT YOUR FOLLOWER.

MOST OF ALL, DELIVER ME FROM THE BONDAGE
OF THE FEAR OF DEATH.

MAKE ME FINALLY UNDERSTAND THAT TO DIE
IN CHRIST IS GAIN.

HELP ME LOOK FORWARD, WITH PRECIOUS
ANTICIPATION, TO MY MOMENT OF ULTIMATE
HEALING.

****

L O V E

LOVE IS THE REALITY, NOT CHANGED BY TIME
OR SPACE.
– Shakti Miller (my friend, healer, and motivator for this
book)

****

AND AS FOR ME…
"I AM ALIVE AND WITHIN ME SHINES A LIGHT
SO BRIGHT IT CAN MAKE ANY DARKNESS GO
AWAY."
– Prem Rawat